P9-DID-099

I LEFT THE LODGE

DALE A. BYERS

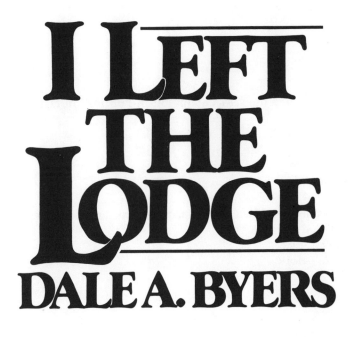

REGULAR BAPTIST PRESS
1300 North Meacham Road
Schaumburg, Illinois 60173-4888

128050

Library of Congress Cataloging-in-Publication Data

Byers, Dale A., 1937-
   I left the lodge/Dale A. Byers.
      p.   cm.
   Bibliography: p.
   ISBN 0-87227-127-7
   1. Freemasonry—Religious aspects—Christianity. 2. Freema-
sons—United States. I. Title.
HS495.B94   1988
366'.1'0973—dc19
                                                  88-31152
                                                    CIP

I LEFT THE LODGE
© 1988
Regular Baptist Press
Schaumburg, Illinois
Printed in U.S.A. All rights reserved

Second printing—1989

Contents

Preface

For many years I have remained silent in regard to the Masonic Lodge. This silence has not been out of fear or shame but out of respect. I have many fine friends and loved ones who belong to the Lodge. It is not my desire to be offensive or harmful to them, but I must speak out on what the Lodge really is. I pray that those Masons who read this book will understand that this is not an attack on them as individuals but rather a disclosure of the organization and the principles upon which it is founded.

I was regularly initiated an Entered Apprentice on August 10, 1958, and passed to the Degree of a Fellow Craft on September 17, 1958, and raised to the Sublime Degree of a Master Mason on September 22, 1958. These events marked my entrance into the Lodge of Free and Accepted Masons in Veedersburg, Indiana, Lodge #491.

The greatest event of my life came, however, in February, 1961, when I surrendered my heart and life to Jesus Christ. Following my conversion I experienced a great struggle regarding my membership in the Lodge. Only after much thought and prayer did I withdraw. I was asked, "Why are you dropping out of the Masons?" Too many times my answer was not the best and lacked the real reason for my action. I would like to answer that question for you today: "Why must the Christian withdraw from the Masonic Lodge?"

Why I Joined the Masons

1

Veedersburg, Indiana, population 2,000, lies twenty miles from the Illinois border. Like most small towns, the residents there are tightly knit. I came from a middle-income family—my father being one of a long line of railroaders. Life at home was sweet and pleasant, and I thank God for the memories of that town. Those people shall always be cherished—they are part of my life, and I hold them dear.

There are certain experiences in our lives we never forget. When I was in my early teens my father, older brother and I began digging a basement under our house. Removing the dirt by wheelbarrow was a laborious undertaking, and my father became seriously ill and spent several months in the hospital. To add to this burden, rains came and the basement began to fill with water, causing the house to settle and begin to sink into the basement hole. The care of two teen sons, a house that was settling into a mudhole and the sickness of her husband placed a tremendous load on my sweet mother.

At this difficult time in my life I was introduced to the Masonic Lodge. I can still picture in my mind the group of men who came into our situation, pumped the water out, jacked the house up, set it on a proper foundation and poured the cement floors for our basement. Words cannot describe what that meant to our family.

My father recovered from his illness, the house remains intact on its foundation, and my brother and I have both matured through the process of raising our families, but that experience is still with me.

From that experience there was a family commitment to the Masonic Lodge. I personally desired to become a Mason, but I was required to wait, since a Mason must be one who is "freeborn, of lawful age, and coming well recommended." The lawful age at that time was twenty-one.

Following high school I met the girl who was to become my wife, and I pledged that my marriage would have the same commitment and happiness that my parents knew. The following July after we were married, I became a man of "lawful age." Applying for Lodge membership, I was regularly initiated an Entered Apprentice the following month, and the next month passed to the Degree of a Fellowcraft. Just a week later I was raised to the Sublime Degree of a Master Mason. Normally it takes several weeks or even months to earn each degree. A Mason once stated that he did not see how I could learn the required materials in such a short time. However, the fact that I did learn it shows how important it was to me. These events marked my entrance into the Lodge of Free and Accepted Masons in Veedersburg, Indiana, Lodge #491.

This might seem to be a good time to end my story and state that "all lived happily evermore." But the best was just beginning. Soon after we were married, my wife asked if we might start attending church, so we tried various churches in the city of Crawfordsville, where we had moved at the time of our wedding. My wife had been a member of Calvary Baptist Church in Danville, Illinois, where she lived prior to our marriage, so we also visited the Pleasant View Baptist Church. The people greeted us warmly. Some of them were employees of R. R. Donnelley Co., where I was an offset printer. Pastor Paul Hubble preached from the Bible with clarity and concern. The message of Jesus Christ was presented, and I was confronted with my need of salvation.

We became regulars at this church and began to see God working in our lives. As a boy I had visited my aunt for a week and attended a Nazarene church with her. There I heard for the first time the gospel and my need to be saved, but I did not come from a church family and there were many things I did not understand. So when Betty and I became regular attenders at the Baptist church it was quite an accomplishment.

One night we attended a revival meeting, and my wife walked to the front of the church and rededicated her life to Christ. She asked the church to pray for her husband. They prayed earnestly and fervently for me, but I did not respond. I felt I could not make a commitment to Christ unless there was some assurance that I could keep and honor the commitment.

Several months passed after my wife's decision to follow Christ. Her example and patience with me made me realize she did have something I needed in my life. There was a hunger in my heart that I could not explain. I would awake often in the night and would sit on the porch smoking and watching the moon sail across the night sky. Several of the workers at Donnelley had witnessed to me of Christ in their lives. I knew they were praying for me.

Finally on a February Sunday morning as the invitation was given to trust Christ as Savior, I closed my hymnal and slipped to the front, where Pastor Hubble shared Bible verses and prayed with me. There was peace and an inner joy at letting God have His way in my life.

We left the church that morning and were enroute to my parents for a birthday dinner for my nephew. There was snow on the ground, and the road up the huge Covington hill west of Crawfordsville was covered with ice. As we approached the crest of a hill, a car going the opposite direction slid sideways into my lane. There was no stopping my little Rambler on those slick roads, and we plowed into the car broadside. This happened less than fifteen minutes after I had trusted Christ!

Pastor Hubble, learning of the accident, came immediately to the scene. I'll never forget his words: "Skip, it's a good thing you got right with God this morning!"

Fortunately there were no major injuries. What God did in my life that day was only a prelude to more blessings. I could not get enough of my Bible, praying or attending church. I am thankful for a pastor who was patient with my elementary questions. I followed the Lord in believer's baptism and grew in the grace and knowledge of Jesus Christ as my Savior.

Some time later Pastor Hubble informed me that some

people had spoken about nominating me for a church office. But there was a clause in the church constitution stating that an officer could not be a member of a secret organization such as the Masonic Lodge. I had read that in the constitution myself and wondered why it was there. He explained some of the Biblical principles involved, prayed with me and left a tract by Dr. Robert T. Ketcham and some other literature about the Lodge.

Words could never describe the turmoil that went on in my heart and mind after this visit. There were three reasons why I thought I could not leave the Lodge. First, there was a love and respect for my father—the one man in my life whom I idealized. He was stronger, wiser, kinder and more joyful than any man I knew. Second, there was a respect and admiration for the men who had taken me into the Lodge. They were men I enjoyed. Third, I was a great debtor to the Lodge. They had come in to help at a time when it seemed no one else would. That strong sense of debt was hardest for me to face. I had not been a member of the Masonic Lodge for very many years, but there was a great depth of commitment.

Only after much thought and prayer did I withdraw and receive my demit. There were many repercussions from my family and friends. Often I was asked, "Why are you dropping out of the Lodge?" This book is an attempt to answer that question.

Freemasonry on the Surface

2

Many people have no knowledge of, or experience with, Masonry. If you are among this group, you need a brief description of the Lodge, a definition of Masonic terms and an explanation of the rites and ceremonies.

Basically the Lodge is a fraternal organization, with secret rites and ceremonies that supposedly teach men good moral principles. The *Indiana Monitor and Freemason's Guide* is a handbook given to each person who becomes a Mason in that state. Other states have their own official Monitors. On pages 7 and 8, the *Indiana Monitor* states:

WHAT IS FREEMASONRY?

For more than two centuries learned craftsmen have ardently sought an accurate, all-inclusive definition for Freemasonry. Our most eminent savants have devoted time, effort and verbiage to the commendable task of expressing in a few, simple words that which is Masonry. Some have almost succeeded. But always, that vital spark which is the very touchstone of our Craft has eluded them.

There is inherent in this ancient and honorable institution an intangible, indefinable element which apparently lies beyond the power of words. Without it, no definition of Masonry can be considered complete.

We may find it impossible to define this elusive component in words, but the understanding Mason knows it is there just as certainly as he knows there is a G.A.O.T.U. He is therefore satisfied to accept at face value one or more of those definitions which, although admittedly incomplete, most closely approach the ideal. Perhaps therein lies one explanation of the power which Masonry exerts upon the hearts of its votaries, who are thus bound together by that "mystic tie" which never the tongue of man shall speak nor the pen of man shall write.

Officially, Masonry is defined as consisting of *a course of moral instruction*, illustrated by types, emblems and allegorical figures. The old English Constitutions state it in this manner, "a system of morality veiled in allegory and illustrated by symbols.". . . Webster says an allegory "represents by suggestive resemblance"; and a symbol is "a visible sign or representation of an idea."

Right Worshipful Brother Charles C. Hunt, Grand Secretary Emeritus of the Grand Lodge of Iowa, A.F. & A.M., proposes the following definition, after an extensive analysis of opinions of other eminent Masonic scholars, *"Freemasonry is an organized society of men symbolically applying the principles of operative masonry and architecture to the science and art of building."* This especially distinguishes our Fraternity from all other organizations which teach a system of morality.

In the March 8, 1987 *Grand Rapids Press*, an entire page was devoted to defining and explaining Freemasonry, written by the *illustrious potentate*, Robert R. Wagner (see Appendix A). There are three basic degrees: the Entered Apprentice, the Fellowcraft and the Master Mason. All three degrees must be obtained before a man is considered a Mason. This group of degrees is known as the "Blue Lodge" because of its universality.

There are various degrees and rites and organizations within Freemasonry, but they are all built upon the foundation of the Blue Lodge. For example, the Eastern Star is a branch of Masonry designed for the participation of both husband and wife. There is the DeMolay for the young men and the Rainbow Girls, Triangle and Job's Daughters for the young ladies.

There are two appendant bodies through which a Master Mason may advance in degrees. They are the York Rite and the Scottish Rite. In the Scottish Rite a Mason may advance to the earned 32d degree. There is also a 33d degree, which is an honorary degree bestowed upon especially worthy Masons who have accomplished outstanding work in such fields as politics and religion. For example, former president Gerald Ford and Norman Vincent Peale are both 33d degree Masons.

In the York Rite, a Master Mason may become a member of three bodies—a chapter of Royal Arch Masons, a council of Royal and Select Masters, and a commandery of Knights Templar. (For more information about the York Rite, see Appendix A.)

The Shriners are well known. When a man reaches the 32d degree in the Scottish Rite or the Knights Templar in the York Rite, he may petition to become a Shriner. Every Shriner is a Mason. (For additional information about the Shriners see Appendix A.)

A key point to remember is that many people have become involved with Freemasonry thinking they have united with only a fraternal organization. If you are considering becoming involved with Freemasonry, be sure you know all the facts.

Freemasonry Beneath the Surface

3

Why cannot a Christian properly belong to an organization that on the surface seems so innocent, so doctrinally neutral, so philanthropic?

My purpose is to demonstrate that Masonry is a part of the system of *this world*, which worships Lucifer and is in opposition and rebellion to the true and living God. This ungodly system is powered, designed and controlled by Satan, who is called "the god of this world" (see 2 Cor. 4:4). There is an ordered system by which Satan controls and manipulates the wicked affairs of men and nations (see Eph. 6:12). Satan manifests himself as an "angel of light" (see 2 Cor. 11:14, 15), giving an appearance of good—but it is only an appearance. Masonry is part of that system. It appears (as does Satan) to be a ministry of light, but it is of spiritual darkness. No amount of good works and social endeavors can conceal the darkness of Masonry. There is more power and influence in this system than most of us are willing to recognize.

For years there has been great speculation concerning the involvement of Freemasonry in governmental affairs of this nation as well as other nations of the world. Consider the markings on the one dollar bill of U.S. currency. On the backside of the dollar bill are two seals of Masonic identification. It cannot be denied that the pyramid with the eye on top is definitely Masonic in origin. The pyramid represents the unfinished Temple, and the eye is symbolic of the "grand architect of the universe." The other seal contains an eagle with its wings spread.

Some have claimed that this eagle had thirty-two feathers on its right wing and thirty-three feathers on the left wing, relating to the earned 32d degree and the honorary 33d degree. It is most clear that there are thirty-two feathers on the right wing, but the thirty-three feathers on the left are not as discernible. The tail of the eagle is well spread, displaying nine feathers which correspond with the nine degrees of the York Rite. Above the head of the eagle is a series of thirteen stars arranged to form the Star of David. King David plays a very significant role in Masonry. There were thirteen colonies which formed the Union, but the number thirteen may also have some Masonic significance. In the eagle's left claw are thirteen arrows and in the eagle's right claw is a branch bearing thirteen berries. Thirteen Masons organized and built the first Shrine temple in 1872, which is the Mecca Temple in New York City. The banner, "e pluribus unum," has also been used in Freemasonry. The motto at the bottom, "novus ordo seclorum" is translated as "a new order of ages" or "new world order."[1] The word *world* comes from the Latin root from which we get "secular," which means world or worldly. This new order is opposed to all that is God's given order.[2]

While it is impossible to prove these symbols have Masonic associations, there have been others who have noticed the obvious connections with Masonry. In 1954, the University of Texas doctoral candidate James David Carter wrote a dissertation ("Freemasonry in Texas: Background, History, and Influence to 1846") that summarized further significance of the Great Seal.[3]

On the front of the dollar bill is a picture of George Washington, who is honored by the Lodge because he was a Mason, as were other U.S. presidents and leaders.[4] (A list of presidents who were Masons is given in Appendix B.) The Masonic Holy Bible gives this picture of the Mason's influence in American history:

Many in the early history of Scotland, England, and France are reported, with reasonable authenticity, to have been Masons. The great majority of the fifty-six signers of the American Declaration of Independence were Masons; George Washington was famed as a Mason; it is authentically reported that most of the generals in the Revolutionary War were Masons; fifteen of the men who have occupied the White House at Washington as presidents have been Masons, and the two others had proposed to unite with the Order, but were overtaken by death before these proposals were carried out. [5]

Whether or not Masonic involvement in our government's affairs can be proved, we must consider the following statement from a 33d degree Mason:

When the Mason learns that the key to the warrior on the block is the proper application of the dynamo of living power, he has learned the mystery of his Craft. The seething energies of Lucifer are in his hands and before he may step onward and upward, he must prove his ability to properly apply [this] energy. [6]

Thus we see the connection between "the god of Masonry" and "the god of this world."

It must be remembered that Masonry is an organism that is universal in scope. Masonry cannot always be measured by what we observe in America. It can be compared with Roman Catholicism which takes on different natures in various countries, depending on its strength. It has been said that Catholicism is a lamb when it is in the minority, a fox when it is in equality and a roaring lion when it is in the majority. Likewise, Masonry has a different nature in various countries. For example, where the occult is more readily accepted you will find Masonry taking on that flavor.

Does all of this sound absurd? Then you do not know the nature of Masonry or the extent and organization of Satan, "the god of this world."

[1] Chuck O'Donnell, *The Standard Handbook of Modern United States Paper Money*, 7th ed., (Iola, WI: Krause Publications, 1982), p. 36.

[2] Ralph Epperson, *Secret Societies*, (Oklahoma City: Southwest Radio Church, n.d.), p. 35.

[3] William Proudstone, *Big Secrets* (New York: William Morrow and Co., 1983), pp. 63, 64.

[4] Rev. C. G. Finney, in *The Character, Claims, and Practical Workings of Freemasonry* (p. 222), quotes a letter from President George Washington, dated Sept. 25, 1798, in which Washington declares he has little to do with the Masonic Lodge.

[5] From the Masonic Holy Bible, according to H. L. Haywood in *Freemasonry and the Bible* (Chicago: The Masonic History Co., 1947), p. 9.

[6] Manly P. Hall, *The Lost Keys of Freemasonry*, (Chicago: The Charles T. Powner Co., 1976), p. 48.

The Roots of Freemasonry

4

To the average person, and to many Masons, the origin of the Lodge would be traced back to 1717, when the first Grand Lodge was organized in the Appletree Tavern in London, England. Also, some people believe Freemasonry has Christian origins. This is totally untrue. The roots of Freemasonry run in a direction opposite Christianity. The Masonic Lodge does not have a Christian foundation.

Roots of Ancient Mystery Religions

Walter L. Wilmhurst, Past Provincial Grand Registrar (West Yorks) is a Masonic author who wrote *The Meaning of Masonry*. He explained that the religions of the Greeks are as important to Masonry as is Christianity, contending that the Greek religions developed the principles of truth and emphasize the mind while the Christian religion developed the heart and emphasized the affections. He very clearly and simply states how Masonry is connected with the Mystery Rites of the East:

> Lastly a chapter has been added upon the important subject which forms the background of the rest—the relationship of modern Masonry to the Ancient Mysteries, from which it is the direct, though greatly attenuated, spiritual descendant.[1]
> It remains with the Craft itself whether it shall enter upon its own heritage as a lineal successor of the Ancient Mysteries and Wisdom-teaching, or whether, by failing

so to do, it will undergo the inevitable fate of everything that is but a form from which its native spirit has departed.[2]

To follow in any detail the course of its history is not now necessary and would require a long treatise. And to do so would also be like following the course of a river backwards from its broad mouth to a point where it becomes an insignificant and scarcely traceable channel. For the race itself has wandered backwards, farther and farther from the original Wisdom-teaching, so that the once broad and bright flood of light upon cosmic principles and the evolution of the human soul has now become contracted into minute points. But that light, like that of a Master Mason, has never been wholly extinguished, however dark the age, and, by the tradition, this of ours is spiritually the darkest of the dark ages. "God has never left Himself without a witness among the children of men," and among the witnesses to the Ancient Wisdom and Mysteries is the system of Masonry; a faint and feeble flicker, perhaps, but nevertheless a true light and in the true line of succession of the primitive doctrine, and one still able to guide our feet into the way of peace and perfection.[3]

Roots of Satan and Worship of Sun God

One of Masonry's recognized historians is H. L. Haywood, who wrote a very interesting article, "A History of Freemasonry." In it he argued that the roots of Freemasonry far precede 1717. Mr. Haywood recognized that many things have contributed to make the Lodge what it is today. He traces Freemasonry through the Operative Masons of the Middle Ages to the Roman Collegian, in which religious and social purposes were combined. Beyond this he traces the roots of the Lodge to the Mystery Religions which emphasized religious experience and finally to the Ancient Religions of the East, primarily that of the worship of the sun.[4]

It is to pagan worship that Masonry must attribute its source. It was through false worship that the Lodge blossomed forth:

It is manifest that Freemasonry has retained heirlooms which in one way or another have come to it out of the abundance of the past. Traces of the earliest form of sun worship are to be found in some of the ceremonials of the Lodge room. Its point within a circle and its five-rayed star were symbols of religious significance in many ancient faiths.[5]

For an example, let us consider the Masonic ceremony of marching around the Lodge room in a circular direction. This practice is called, "circumambulation," which symbol is a point within a circle. Mr. Haywood considers it a root of sun worship:

> The rite of circumambulation, as a certain mystical journey about a Lodge room as technically described may be mentioned as a conspicuous example. Circumambulation is very old and well nigh universal. The Egyptians used it in their cult practice carrying images of Isis or Osiris around their temples and altars.[6]
> Circumambulation is thus a product of sun worship.[7]

The worship of the sun is not viewed by Freemasonry as false worship but rather as part of the evolutionary process of religion. Haywood wrote:

> Apollo is the sun, Mithra is the sun, Osiris is the sun, Balder is the sun, and although each of these pagan deities had other attributes, they belong to a universal solar mythology, the existence of which constitutes a set of facts the historian must ponder well if he is rightly to understand the unfolding of human faith.[8]

Instances of sun worship are recorded in the Bible, and God always condemns it and commands His people to forsake it. One of the best examples is that of Baal worship. Baal was one of the false gods of the Canaanites, also called Bab, Belu or Bel.[9] In Numbers 25, we find that God brought death upon 24,000 Israelites for participating in sun worship. One of the most significant examples of sun worship is at the Tower of Babel. It is interesting to note that the men at the Tower of Babel did not profess to be atheists but rather embraced a conglomeration of heathenistic principles of worship. Is it any wonder it was called "Babel," which means "confusion"? There is a close connection between Babel and Babylon—symbolic Babylon represents a system which is anti-Christ in nature. For example, in Revelation 17:5 we find words of judgment upon the false system of morality:

> And upon her forehead was a name written, MYS-TERY, BABYLON THE GREAT, THE MOTHER OF HARLOTS AND ABOMINATIONS OF THE EARTH.

It is most significant that Masonic writings connect Freemasonry with Babel. The "Old Charges," early writings of Freemasonry, included the Regius Poem or the Halliwell Manuscript, one of the earliest writings.[10] One version of this manuscript ties in Freemasonry with the Tower of Babel:

> This is followed by another version of the origin of the Craft, which purports to trace its history from the Deluge to the Tower of Babel.[11]

The circumambulation also represents the horrible immorality that characterized the religions of Egypt, Babylon and other false systems of worship. Prostitution and sex were a basic part of their temple life. Albert Mackey, one of Masonry's most respected authors, wrote in *Mackey's Masonic Ritualist*:

> The point within a circle is an interesting and important symbol in Freemasonry. . . . The symbol is really a beautiful but somewhat abstruse allusion to the old sun-worship, and introduces us for the first time to that modification of it known among the ancients as the worship of the Phallus.
> The Phallus was an imitation of the male generative organ. It was represented usually by a column, which was surrounded by a circle at its base, intented for the cteis, or female generative organ. This union of the phallus and the cteis, which is well represented by the point

within the circle, was intended by the ancients as a type of the prolific powers of nature, which they worshipped under the united form of the active or male principle, and the passive or female principle.[12]

Mackey also states from *Mackey's Masonic Lexicon*:

The phallus was the wooden image of the membrum verile, which being affixed to a pole, formed a part of most of the pagan mysteries, and was worshipped as the emblem of the male generative principle. The phallic worship was first established in Egypt. . . . From Egypt it was introduced into Greece, and its exhibition formed a part of the Dionysian mysteries. In the Indian mysteries, it was called lingam, and was always found in the most holy place of the temple.[13]

The Lodge Room

All Masonic temples are constructed to run east and west. The Master of the Lodge "resides" in the east—the sun rises in the east. Above his head on the eastern wall is a large letter "G." There are no officers seated on the north side of the Lodge room. (See Appendix C for an actual illustration of a Lodge room.) William Schnoebelen wrote in *Freemasonry— Satan's Flytrap?*:

The Letter "G": In the Fellowcraft (2d) degree, the candidate is taught that the letter "G" is exalted before every Masonic lodge because of two reasons: it is the initial of geometry, and it is the initial of the "Sacred Name of Deity."

Interestingly, the "Sacred Name of Deity" is never spoken in the Blue Lodge, but the candidate is left to assume that the word referred to is "God." There are some problems with this. First of all, "God" is not the God of the Bible's name. It is a generic title, which is translated from the Hebrew EL or the Greek THEOS. Both these terms can be applied to either God or false gods. The name of the God of the Bible is YHUH, usually translated Yahweh, or Jehovah. It does not begin with "G" but with the Hebrew letter "Yod."

It therefore becomes apparent that the "G" could stand for either the true God or the many false gods. You may say that is quibbling. Few Masons, you say, are Hebrew scholars. Perhaps, but remember, Masonry is essentially an import. Long before it was practiced in America, it was done in England, France, Italy and Germany. Today it is in virtually every country in the Free World. In few of these countries does God's name begin with "G." It begins with "D" in France, Italy, and Spain, for example.

What few Masons know, and even fewer will tell you, is the "G" stands for the "Sacred Name" of the Great Initiator of Blue Lodge masonry: the mysterious figure who presides in the North of the Lodge. Think about it—did you ever consider why there is no officer in the North?

Most Masons, if they've bothered to think of the question at all, will tell you there are no windows in the northern wall of the temple; therefore, that wall is referred to as the place of Masonic darkness. Of course in magic, the northern quarter of the circle represents the sun at midnight, so it is also dark in that system. More importantly, in witchcraft, the North is the place from which come the Great Lords of the Outer Spaces, among them the Horned Lord Lucifer and his emissaries.

Now Lucifer is too smart to let his name be well-known, even among Masons. In the occult, his chief ambassador is the one who presides in the North; and in most continental Masonic temples, there is a throne left vacant for this ambassador, especially in the L'Droit Humaine lodges, the OTO lodges, the Martiniste/Masonic lodges, and the Palladium lodges. Who is this mystery figure? The celebrated Compte de St. Germaine is the person who is felt to preside from the North over every meeting of Freemasons. His name means "Holy Brother", and begins with "G." What is so bad about him? He is supposedly hundreds of years old, keeping himself alive through alchemy and masonic science. Literally dozens of occult and New Age orders identify him as the replacement for Jesus Christ as the new "messiah" of the Aquarian age. Satanists regard him as Satan's right hand man on earth; the literal embodiment of satanic puissance! He is supposedly the earthly head of the Ancient and Illuminated Seers of Bavaria (the infamous Illuminati). He is, dear Christian brothers, the one whom the letter

"G" represents, before whom all the Masons must humbly bow.[14]

In conclusion, if we could find one single root of Masonry we would find it in the heart of Satan who, from the beginning of earth, has attempted to thwart the worship of the true and living God by creating systems of false worship, whether it be the Tower of Babel or the rituals of Freemasonry.

Albert Pike, a well-known author of Freemasonry, connected Masonry and Luciferian worship:

> To you, Sovereign Grand Inspectors General, we say this, that you may repeat it to the Brethren of the 32nd, 31st, and 30th degrees—the Masonic Religion should be, by all of us initiates of the high degrees, maintained in the purity of the Luciferian Doctrine.[15]

[1] W. L. Wilmhurst, *The Meaning of Masonry* (New York: Bell Publishing Co., 1980), p. 7.

[2] Ibid., p. 216.

[3] Ibid., p. 178.

[4] H. L. Haywood, *A History of Freemasonry* (New York: The John Day Co., 1927), n.p.

[5] Ibid., p. 17.

[6] Ibid., p. 39.

[7] Ibid., p. 41.

[8] Ibid., p. 21.

[9] *International Standard Bible Encyclopedia*, Vol., 1, p. 345.

[10] H. L. Stillson, *A History of the Ancient and Honorable Fraternity of Free and Accepted Masons and Concordant Orders* (Boston: The Fraternity Publishing Co., 1912), p. 65.

[11] Haywood, *"History of Freemasonry,"* p. 21.

[12] A. G. Mackey, *Mackey's Masonic Ritualist*, pp. 62, 63.

[13] A. G. Mackey, *Mackey's Masonic Lexicon*, p. 353.

[14] William Schnoebelen, *Freemasonry—Satan's Flytrap?* (Dubuque: Aletheia Ministries, n,d.), pp. M9-11.

[15] J. E. Decker, Jr., *The Question of Freemasonry* (Issaquah, WA: Free the Masons Ministry, n.d.), p. 6.

The Masonic View of the Bible 5

The Bible is the verbally inspired and inerrant Word of God, and it is the only such book.

In the Scriptures God reveals His will to all mankind. Human reasoning does not have greater authority than the Word of God. Human reasoning changes and is fallible; God's Word is eternal (see Ps. 119:89). Therefore, if God speaks out against anything, we must take His words seriously. We may ask, "Are there principles of the Bible that are contrary to the Masonic Lodge?"

> All scripture is given by inspiration of God, and is profitable for doctrine, for reproof, for correction, for instruction in righteousness: that the man of God may be perfect, throughly furnished unto all good works (2 Tim. 3:16, 17).

> Knowing this first, that no prophecy of the scripture is of any private interpretation. For the prophecy came not in old time by the will of man: but holy men of God spake as they were moved by the Holy Ghost (2 Pet. 1:20, 21).

The Kabalah is a book of ancient Jewish mysticism and magic that originated in the 12th or 13th century. It is an occult deviation which the Hebrew people have totally repudiated. Albert Pike, in *Morals and Dogma of the Ancient and Accepted Scottish Rite of Freemasonry*, stated:

> All truly dogmatic religions have issued from the Kabalah and return to it. Everything scientific and grand in

the religious dreams of the Illuminati, Jacob Boehme, Swedenborg, Saint-Martin, and others is borrowed from the Kabalah; all the Masonic associations owe to it their secrets and their symbols.[1]

The Kabalah alone consecrates the Alliance of the Universal Reason and the Divine Word. . . .[2]

Many Masons believe that the Lodge does not deny the authority of the Scriptures, for they say that Masonry is built on the Bible.[3] However, the Lodge's own teaching is that it, as an institution, rejects the authority of the Bible as the only God-given book. To the Lodge the Bible means nothing more than the Koran, Vedas or any other book of other religions.[4] Here is what Masonry says concerning the Bible in the Lodge:

The volume of the Sacred Law is an indispensable part of the furniture of a Lodge. In our jurisdiction it is usually the Bible, but any candidate not a Christian may have substituted for it any other volume he considers sacred; e.g., the Old Testament, Koran, Vedas or Laws of Confucious.[5]

Contrary to this view, the Bible is exclusive—it alone has God's stamp of approval. To elevate other books to a position equal with the Bible is to clearly reject the Bible's teaching. To Masonry, the Bible is not the authority but merely a symbol, the same as the square and compass in their emblem.

Freemasonry has no sacred book of its own. In our jurisdiction it adopts the Bible as a symbol of all sacred books.[6]

Obviously, if other books are able to replace the Bible, the Lodge cannot be built on the Bible. And, if the Bible is regarded as purely symbolic, the Lodge has denied the authority of the Scriptures, for the Bible speaks in reality. In the ceremonies of the Lodge, the square and compass lie *on top* of the Bible. This is a true picture of the Masonic chain of authority—the Lodge above, the Bible below.[7]

When the Scriptures are used in the Lodge, they are misquoted and misused, and thus Masonry shames the true teachings of the Bible and dishonors Jesus Christ. The Masonic Lodge does not use the name of Jesus Christ in prayer or when using the Scriptures, as this might offend a brother Mason who is not a Christian. For example, 1 Peter 2:5 states, "Ye also, as lively stones, are built up a spiritual house, an holy priesthood, to offer up spiritual sacrifices, acceptable to God by Jesus Christ." When the Lodge uses this verse in the Mark Master degree, which is the first degree of the York Rite, they omit the words, "by Jesus Christ." This completely alters the verse's meaning. What is actually being done is turning the Bible into a lie by making it say something that it does not; namely, that a man has an approach to God apart from Jesus Christ.[8] (See *Mackey's Masonic Ritualist*, p. 271.)

Another example of the Masonic practice of misusing the Scriptures is that of exchanging words to suit its own purpose. Hebrews 9:27 states, "And as it is appointed unto men once to die, but after this the judgment." Listen to how this verse is misquoted: "It is appointed to all men once to die and after death comes the resurrection."[9]

There is a great deal of difference between the words *resurrection* and *judgment*. The Lodge ignores sin and judgment and thus misquotes and misrepresents the Scriptures to fit its own teaching.

Masonry also spiritualizes the Bible by making Biblical references to a Christian refer to Masons instead. First Corinthians 6:15–20 has a great deal to say about men being the temples of God. It is explained quite clearly that Christians, and Christians only, are the temples which are indwelt by the Holy Spirit. But Masonry teaches that being a Christian is not the determining factor in being a temple of God. In the *Indiana Monitor and Freemason's Guide* there are several definitions given to Masonry; and then follows this quote:

> Combine the above definitions, if you will. Add to them that cosmic spark which makes of man a Temple of God; and you will be as close as mortal may ever come to defining our gentle Craft with words.[10]

Can anyone honestly say that it was through the Masonic Lodge that he was made a temple of God, or must it be through the New Birth that takes place only through saving faith in Christ as Savior? These are three samples of Masonic methods of using the Scriptures, but they clearly show how God's Word is used to their own design.

> And if any man shall take away from the words of the book of this prophecy, God shall take away his part out of the book of life, and out of the holy city, and from the things which are written in this book (Rev. 22:19).

[1] Decker, *The Question of Freemasonry*, p. 10.

[2] Ibid.

[3] Ibid.

[4] Haywood, *Freemasonry and the Bible*, p. 13. "The real 'bible' of the Operative Lodges of the Middle Ages was a copy of the Old Charges."

[5] Lawrence R. Taylor, *Indiana Monitor and Freemason's Guide* (IN: Grand Lodge of Indiana, 1957), p. 38.

[6] Ibid., p. 40.

[7] Rev. Harmon Taylor, former 32d Degree Mason and former New York State Grand Chaplain, testifies he witnessed the Bible being replaced with the Koran in Wadsworth Lodge #417. We must then assume that the *only* thing that must be on the altar is the square and compass, symbols of the Phallic Religion.

[8] Alva J. McClain, *Freemasonry and Christianity* (IN: Brethren Missionary Herald Co., n.d.) See also, *A Frank Exposure of Freemasonry*, National Christian Association, Chicago.

[9] Homer F. Newton, *Michigan Monitor and Ceremonies*, p. 86.

[10] Taylor, *Indiana Monitor*, p. 8.

Freemasonry Is a Religion

6

Is Freemasonry a religion? Yes, according to its leading writers. J. M. Ward wrote in *Freemasonry—Its Aims and Ideals:*

> I boldly aver that freemasonry is a religion, yet it no way conflicts with any other religion, unless that religion holds that no one outside its portals can be saved.[1]

Pike, in *The Morals and Dogma of the Ancient and Accepted Scottish Rite of Freemasonry*, wrote:

> Every Masonic Temple is a Temple of Religion, and its teachings are instruction in religion.[2]

He also wrote:

> It [Masonry] is the universal, eternal, immutable religion, such as God planted it in the heart of universal humanity. No creed has ever been long-lived that has not built on this foundation. It is the base and they are the superstructure.[3]

Here are some additional statements that reveal Masonry as a religion:

> Therefore no private piques or quarrels must be brought within the Door of the Lodge, far less any quarrels about religion, or Nations or State Policy, we being only as Masons of the universal religion above mentioned.[4]

In this statement we see that Masonry is a religion of Universalism. Universalism basically is that teaching which says that all individuals of every faith will go to Heaven—some by way of Christianity, some by way of Muhammadanism, Buddhism, good works or any other way of one's own choosing. Here is another quote which verifies Masonry as Universalism:

> This founded modern Speculative Masonry on the rock of non-sectarianism and the brotherhood of all men who believe in a common Father regardless of His name, His church, or the way in which He is worshipped. . . .[5]

Notice two things in the above quote:

First the terms "Fatherhood of God" and "Brotherhood of all men" are misused. Many religious people do not have fellowship with God as a son with a father. Sin is a barrier. Jesus said to the Jews of that day (the most religious group of people who ever walked the face of the earth), "Ye are of your father the devil" (John 8:44). God is the Creator and Master of all; but when mankind was plunged into sin, fellowship with God was completely severed. Fellowship with God is restored only through Jesus Christ, Who paid the full price for our sins on the cross. While all individuals are creatures of God through creation, not all individuals are children of God by redemption. We are able to enter into fellowship with the Father only through the mediatorial work of Christ. "For there is one God, and one mediator between God and men, the man Christ Jesus" (1 Tim. 2:5).

Second, notice that the Masonic Lodge is founded on the concept that the way in which God is worshiped is of no importance. This is completely contrary to the teachings of the Bible from the beginning to the end. The Old Testament stresses the necessity to approach God in the proper manner. This was in preparation for the coming of His Son. God's standard has not changed, neither the method of approach— it is through the blood alone that we can worship Him. Hebrews 9:12 states, "Neither by the blood of goats and calves, but by his own blood he entered in once into the holy place, having obtained eternal redemption for us."

One of Masonry's most competent scholars was Dr. Albert G. Mackey, who authored such Masonic materials as *A Lexicon of Free Masonry, Marvel of the Lodge, The Book of the Chapter, A Textbook of Masonic Jurisprudence, Cryptic Masonry, The Symbolism of Masonry, The Masonic Ritualist* and finally, the crowning work of his life, which took thirty years in preparation, *The Encyclopedia of Freemasonry*.[6] In it he wrote:

> Look at its ancient landmarks, its sublime ceremonies, its profound symbols and allegories—all inculcating religious doctrine, commanding religious truth, and who can deny that it is eminently a religious institution?[7]
>
> Masonry, then, is indeed a religious institution; and on this ground mainly, if not alone, should the religious Mason defend it.[8]

The Masonic Lodge is thus openly declared to be a religious institution in purpose. Further evidence of Masonry's belief of Universalism is seen in an article entitled, "Freemasonry and the Bible":

> After the first (or Mother) grand Lodge was constituted it wrote into its book of Constitutions a famous paragraph entitled, "Concerning God and Religion" in which it laid it down as a law that though in ancient times Masons were expected to be of the religion which belonged to the country in which they lived, they were henceforth to be required only to belong to that religion in which all good men are agreed.[9]

It is interesting to note that this statement does not speak of "those religions," but rather of "that religion" in which all good men are agreed. Again we turn to the *Indiana Monitor* in a little section entitled, "When Is a Man a Mason?":

> A man is a Mason, "When he finds good in every faith that helps any man lay hold of divine things, that sees majestic meanings in life, whatever the name of that faith may be."[10]

This should remove any doubt that Universalism is the thrust of Masonry. There is only one faith that will ever help men to lay hold of divine things: personal faith in Jesus Christ and His finished work on the cross. Every other religion is a counterfeit by Satan to drag man's soul to hell, even if it is the respected name of Masonry. The religion of Masonry is Universalism, and there should be no fellowship with that kind of unbelief!

The terms and the names that Masonry uses reveal its true purpose. One of the main functions of the Lodge is "worship." The Lodge considers itself to be a worshipful Lodge. When the candidate takes the oaths, he begins by saying, "I, (candidate's name), in the presence of Almighty God, this worshipful Lodge. . . ." If members deny that the Lodge has a religious purpose, why do Masons consider the Lodge as worshipful? The buildings in which the meetings are held are usually called temples, not simply lodge halls. Are not temples for the purpose of worship? Every lodge meeting must be opened and closed with prayer. The names of the officers are also significant: the Worshipful Master, Junior and Senior Deacons, and so on. These names are all connected with worship. Some of the titles are blasphemous to Christ. For example, there is an officer of the Shriners entitled, "The Potentate." Webster's Seventh New Collegiate Dictionary defines a potentate as "one who wields controlling power; sovereign." The Bible teaches us that Christ alone is the Potentate; therefore, He alone is to be the controlling force of the Christian's life. When Christ returns to earth the second time, He will come to rule the entire world: "Until the appearing of our Lord Jesus Christ: Which in His times He shall shew, who is the blessed and only Potentate, the King of kings, and Lord of lords" (1 Tim. 6:14, 15).

Any group that teaches a way of worshiping God and presents a plan for getting to Heaven must be classified as being a religion. In Masonry, the way of salvation is through good works, and evidently union with the Masonic Lodge merits a man as being worthy of Heaven, for Masons are taught they are going to be resurrected to that glorious, heavenly lodge.

As we noted earlier, there are three separate ceremonies that a candidate must go through in order to become a Mason. Each degree has a specific message and is symbolic of some higher teaching. The first degree, the "Entered Apprentice," begins with having the candidate blindfolded and dressed in the special garment for that degree. The initiate must remove all metallic substances, including his wedding ring. He is led about the room with a rope around his neck. It is the degree which symbolizes infancy and the entrance into the realm of Masonry.

> The Entered Apprentice is the child in Freemasonry. The lessons which he receives are simply intended to cleanse the heart and prepare the recipient for that mental illumination which is to be given in the next degree.[11]

The second degree, "Fellowcraft," concerns itself with the "working tools," learning how to live and work with the tools of operative Masons—the plumb, square and level. This degree symbolizes the preparation for a future life, using these instruments in a spiritual sense.

> This degree, therefore, by fitting emblems, is intended to typify man laboring amid all the difficulties that encumber the beginner in the attainment of learning and science; the struggles of the ardent mind for the attainment of truth—and above all, Divine Truth, the comprehension of which, standing in the Middle Chamber, after his laboring ascent of the winding stairs, he can only approximate by the reception of an imperfect and yet glorious reward, in revelation of that "hieroglyphic light which none but Craftsman ever saw."[12]

The third degree is the Master Mason's Degree, or "Sublime Degree." This degree is the most significant in regard to eternity, death and the resurrection, as the name implies.

> The Sublime Degree teaches that in another life it may be found. That is why it is the Sublime Degree.[13]

In the ceremony of the Third Degree, the candidate, blind-folded and dressed in his special garment for that degree, is led around the room with a cabletow or rope wrapped three times around his body. The candidate is then the main character in a skit in which the Lodge reenacts the story of Hiram Abiff who, as Grand Master, was attacked by three ruffians—Jubela, Jubelo and Jubelum. The three different attacks are all to obtain the secrets invested in him. His refusal to divulge the secret word results in his being struck with a fatal blow to the forehead. The plot that follows involves the burial of the body of Hiram Abiff by the ruffians and search for his body by the workers. The body is found, and the three ruffians are apprehended. Two unsuccessful attempts are made to raise the body from the grave. First, an assembly of Entered Apprentices is sent out to the task, but the attempts are futile. Second, an assembly of Fellowcraft is sent, but they, too, fail to raise the dead body of Hiram Abiff from the grave. It is not until an assembly of Master Masons is sent that success is accomplished. The last procedure in the ceremony is that of the resurrection. The candidate is given the Master Mason's grip, called the Lion's Paw, and is resurrected from the dead to new life and fellowship with the Lodge.

Every Christian should withdraw from the Lodge, if for no other reason than the picture of the Third Degree and the resurrection. The truth is that there will be a resurrection of every individual, but only the true Christian will be resurrected to a sublime life; all others will go to eternal torment. (See John 5:28, 29; Rev. 20:11–15.) The symbolic resurrection of the Masonic candidate is a counterfeit of the resurrection with the Christian. Another interesting point is the name of the grip with which the candidate is brought to new life—the "Lion's Paw." Jesus Christ is called the Lion of Judah in Revelation 5:5 and also in several passages in the Old Testament. Only through Him can we have that hope of eternal bliss:

> O death, where is thy sting? O grave, where is thy victory? The sting of death is sin; and the strength of sin is the law. But thanks be to God, which giveth us the victory through our Lord Jesus Christ (1 Cor. 15:55–57).

Masonry's doctrine of eternity may also be illustrated by its "Esoteric Emblems."

> The first three of these are striking emblems of mortality and afford serious reflections to a thinking mind; but they would be still more gloomy were it not for the Sprig of Acacia. . . which serves to remind us of that imperishable part of man which survives the grave, and bears the nearest affinity to the supreme intelligence which pervades all nature, and which can never, never, never die. Then finally, my brethren, let us imitate...; that, like him, we may welcome the grim tyrant Death, and receive him as a kind messenger sent by our Supreme Grand Master, to translate us from this imperfect to that all-perfect, glorious, and celestial Lodge above, where the Supreme Architect of the Universe presides.[14]

The ceremonies and the symbols reveal that Masonry definitely does teach the doctrine of eternity.

So the question must be asked, What must be done in order for an individual to gain admission into Heaven? The same question was asked by the Philippian jailer in Acts 16:30 when he fell before the apostle Paul and Silas crying, "What must I do to be saved?" The Christian can only answer as did Paul: "Believe on the Lord Jesus Christ, and thou shalt be saved." Faith in Jesus as personal Savior is the only channel and only requirement for obtaining Heaven (see John 3:16; Rom. 5:1). This, however, is not the answer of Masonry, as outlined in the following words:

> Then by the benefit of a pass, a pure and blameless life with a firm reliance on Divine Providence, shall we gain ready admission into that celestial Lodge above where the Supreme Architect of the Universe presides; where standing at the right of our Supreme Grand Master, He will be pleased to pronounce us just and upright Masons; then will we be fitly prepared as living stones for that spiritual building, that house not made with hands eternal in the heavens; where no discordant voice shall be heard, but all the soul shall experience shall be perfect

bliss, and all it shall express will be perfect praise; and love divine will ennoble every heart, and hosannas exalted employ every tongue.[15]

According to this quote the resurrection of the Mason will be to that heavenly lodge, but how are such blessings obtained? Masonry claims it is through the "benefit of the pass." In other words, before an individual is permitted into the Lodge room he must first produce the secret word or sign. This is called the "pass" and is revealed only to Masons; therefore, outsiders are not able to gain admission. Likewise, the above words state that Masonry also claims to have the "pass" to the heavenly lodge. How contrary this is to the teaching of the Bible. Only through the shed blood of Jesus Christ can admission into Heaven be gained. The above quote also states that, as Masons, they will be readily admitted into Heaven and pronounced "just" and properly "fitted and prepared." Is this what the Bible teaches? No! Indeed not! Galatians 2:21 states, "I do not frustrate the grace of God: for if righteousness come by the law, then Christ is dead in vain." What a horrible thought to think that Christ died in vain. If there had been any way of getting to Heaven other than through the cross, God would not have allowed His Only Begotten Son to be slain at Calvary. If the Masonic Lodge could accomplish for a soul the way to Heaven, then Christ suffered the agony of all hell in vain. His was a worthless and useless death if the Lodge's plan for getting to Heaven is true.

Further evidence of the Masonic method of salvation is viewed in the following portion:

By its legend and all its ritual, it is implied that we have been redeemed from the death of sin and the sepulchre of pollution.[16]

The word *redeem* or *redemption* has the meaning of being delivered from something by the payment of a price. The Masonic teaching mentions redemption from death; but who is the redeemer, and who has paid the price for the release of that soul? It is implied in the Third Degree that the Lodge has redeemed the Mason from death and given him hope for the resurrection and blessing of God. What a tragedy that men should trust something as hopeless as Masonry, and how wonderful for the Christian who can turn to 1 Peter 1:18 and 19 and be able to say with full assurance, "What a wonderful Savior!"

Forasmuch as ye know that ye were not redeemed with corruptible things, as silver and gold, from your vain conversation received by tradition from your fathers; but with the precious blood of Christ, as of a lamb without blemish and without spot.

[1] Quoted in H. R. Taylor's *Freemasonry—A Grand Chaplain Speaks Out* (Issaquah, WA: Free the Masons Ministry, n.d.), p. 4.

[2] A. Pike, *The Morals and Dogma of the Ancient and Accepted Scottish Rite of Freemasonry* (WA: House of the Temple, 1966), p. 213.

[3] Ibid., p. 219.

[4] Lawrence R. Taylor, *Indiana Monitor*, p. 32.

[5] Ibid., p. 19.

[6] Dr. Alva J. McClain considers this work in greater detail in his book, *Freemasonry and Christianity*.

[7] Albert G. Mackey, *The Encyclopedia of Freemasonry* (New York: The Masonic History Co., 1910), n.p.

[8] Ibid.

[9] Ibid.

[10] Taylor, *Indiana Monitor*, n.p.

[11] Ibid., p. 137.

[12] Ibid., p. 139.

[13] Ibid., p. 148.

[14] Ibid., pp. 106, 107.

[15] Homer F. Newton, *Michigan Monitor and Ceremonies*, p. 42.

[16] Taylor, *Indiana Monitor*, p. 145.

Masonic Symbols Betray Christ 7

Have you ever wondered, perhaps from childhood, what the various symbols of Masonry mean? Perhaps you saw some of them hanging on the door of their meeting place, or perhaps you saw one of the symbols on a member's ring. Symbolism is very important to Masonry:

> The symbol of Masonry is the soul of Masonry. Every symbol of a lodge is a religious teacher, the mute teacher also of morals and philosophy.[1]

But, wait a minute! A *religious* teacher? Isn't Masonry merely a social organization? Charles H. Claudy, a Masonic author, says:

> Take from Masonry its symbols and but the husks remain, the kernel is gone. He who hears but the words of Freemasonry misses their meaning entirely.[2]

The symbols of Masonry are for the purpose of teaching religious content, and it is too openly declared to be denied.[3] Here are some examples:

The Masonic Apron

The white cloth that the Mason wears is an "apron." It must be worn whenever the Lodge is meeting. Consider the words of the ceremony in which it is presented to the candidate:

The lambskin, or white leather apron is an emblem of innocence, and the badge of a Mason more ancient than the Golden Fleece or Roman Eagle; more honorable than the Star and Garter, or any other order that could be conferred upon you at this time or any future period by king, prince, potentate, or any other person, except he be a Mason; I hope you will wear it with equal pleasure to yourself and honor to the fraternity.[4]

These words are a disavowal of Jesus Christ and the plain teaching of the Bible. The most significant fact of the above quote is that a lamb was used and that the apron is a clothing of innocence. Jesus Christ was the Lamb of God slain for the sins of the world. Only He is the emblem of innocence. The white lambskin apron is a counterfeit for the righteousness of Christ which robes the Christian. The Masonic Lodge gives its members a false assurance they will stand as innocent before God. In the last part of the "Apron Ceremony" we find these words:

And when at last your weary feet shall have reached the end of their toilsome journey, and from your nerveless grasp shall forever drop the working tools of life, may the record of your life and conduct be as pure and spotless as this fair emblem which I now place within your hands.

And when your soul shall stand naked and alone before the Great White Throne, may it be your lot, my brother, to hear from Him Who sitteth there as Judge Supreme, the welcome words, "Well done, good and faithful servant, enter thou into the joy of the Lord."[5]

Thus the Masonic Lodge usurps Christ and gives a false hope to those who wear the Masonic Apron. Let us understand the true purpose of the Great White Throne found in Revelation 20:11–15. There are no words of blessing and reward at the Great White Throne; only words of condemnation. No Christian will ever stand before, and be judged at, the Great White Throne. It is here that those *without* Christ will be judged and condemned to the eternal lake of fire and torment. Instead of "Well done, good and faithful servant," there will be the words, "Depart from me, ye cursed." The Lodge has again misused the Word of God.

Also, there will never be even one record of an individual's life as being pure and spotless. God's Word says, "All have sinned, and come short of the glory of God" (Rom. 3:23). All men need the Savior, and a Christian must separate himself from any organization which allows for the belief that Christ is not the only way to Heaven.

The Masonic Light

The context of the ceremonies themselves add even more influence to Masonic symbols. When the Entered Apprentice is brought into the Lodge he is asked, "In whom do you put your trust?" The candidate must answer, "In God." From the very beginning, the candidate is made aware that what follows is of religious content. He is brought to the altar upon which lie the three greater lights of Masonry: the Bible, the square and the compass. The three lesser lights are the sun, moon and the Worshipful Master of the Lodge. The candidate is asked what he most desires, and he replies, "Light." The blindfold is then removed from his eyes so he can observe the lights of Masonry. The symbolism is of one being in spiritual darkness and then being brought to light by the Masonic Lodge. How contrary to the teaching of the Scriptures! Jesus said, "I am the light of the world: he that followeth me shall not walk in darkness, but shall have the light of life" (John 8:12). After Christ has opened a person's sin-blinded eyes, why should the person remain united with an organization in spiritual darkness?

The "light of Masonry" is not the "Light of the Bible." Christ is the Light, and Satan gives but an appearance of light. The light of the Bible is truth that flows from a heart of love; the light of Masonry is deceit that flows from Satan.

The glorious privileges of a Master Mason are in keeping with his greater knowledge and wisdom. For him the heavens have opened, and the Great Light has bathed him in its radiance. The prodigal son, so long a wanderer in the regions of darkness, has returned to his

Father's house. The voice speaks from the Heavens, its power thrilling the Master until his own being seems filled with its divinity, says, "This is my beloved Son, in whom I am well pleased." He (the Master Mason) in truth has become the spokesman of the Most High. He stands between the glowing fire light and the world. Through him passes HYDRA, the great snake, and from its mouth there pours to man the light of God.[6]

Kissing the Bible

Too many people are fooled by sentimentalism, and they seem to think anything that appears to be pious and reverent is pleasing to God. The Mason is required to kneel and kiss the Bible (or Koran or other holy book). What an appearance this gives of subjection to it. How shameful it is that the Masonic Lodge does not submit to what the Bible teaches. A kiss is not always an act of love; it has also been an act of betrayal. Judas betrayed Christ with a kiss; likewise the Masonic Lodge betrays Jesus Christ with their ceremonial kiss for they deny the necessity of His atoning blood. The Bible is to them merely a book printed on paper, the same as any modern-day novel or science fiction story. The difference is in what it says and teaches. A love for God's Word is not revealed by ceremonial kissing; it is evidenced by a godly and Holy Spirit-filled life which is available only to the born-again Christian.

The Masonic Doctrine of the New Birth

From the preface of Wilmhurst's book, *The Meaning of Freemasonry*, come these significant lines:

> Wilmhurst carefully places his designs upon the trestleboard to build his thesis that the alpha and omega of Freemasonry is not the repetition of the ritual nor the safeguarding of secrets, but the regeneration of the Brethren.[7]

The beginning and the end of Freemasonry is to give regeneration to the Mason. (See also *Interesting Facts about Freemasonry*, p. 21.)

In contrast, the Bible teaches that it is only those who place their faith in Jesus Christ as Lord and Savior who receive the New Birth. Recorded in John 3 is Jesus' talk with Nicodemus:

There was a man of the Pharisees, named Nicodemus, a ruler of the Jews: The same came to Jesus by night, and said unto him, Rabbi, we know that thou art a teacher come from God: for no man can do these miracles that thou doest, except God be with him. Jesus answered and said unto him, Verily, verily, I say unto thee, Except a man be born again, he cannot see the kingdom of God (John 3:1–3).

Notice three things about Nicodemus. First, he was a Pharisee. He was associated with one of the most religious groups of people who walked the face of the earth. He was an extremely religious man.

Second, he was a ruler of the Jews. As a member of the Sanhedrin, he held a most prestigious position. It was a position that was coveted, admired and respected by his own peers and friends.

Third, he said such nice things about Jesus. He said, "You are a man come from God, for no mere man can do these miracles." From a human perspective, if we saw a man who was extremely religious, well respected among his fellow men, and who said great things about Jesus Christ, we would say he was ready for Heaven. However, Jesus did not view Nicodemus as such. Jesus said to him, "Unless a man is born again, he cannot enter into the kingdom of God." We are instructed from God's Word that we are born again only by trusting Jesus Christ as Savior. This is made clear in John 1:12, 13. The New Birth is that work of the Holy Spirit which regenerates life to a person who has been dead spiritually.

The Masonic doctrine of regeneration is best illustrated through the Holy Royal Arch Degree, which follows the less advanced degrees. The Holy Royal Arch Degree symbolized what is called "the Doctrine of Exaltation." It is here that Satan has counterfeited the Christian experience of the New Birth.

In W. L. Wilmhurst's book, *The Meaning of Masonry*, we have the following:

The completeness of regeneration theoretically pos-
tulated in those four stages is marked, it should be ob-
served, by the very significant expression used in connection with a Royal Arch Chapter, which is interpreted
as meaning "My people, having obtained mercy," which
in its further analysis signifies that all the parts and facul-
ties ("people") of the candidate's organism have at last,
and as the result of his previous discipline and ordeals,
become sublimated and integrated in a new quality and
higher order of life than that previously enjoyed in virtue of his merely temporal nature. In a word, he has become regenerated. He has achieved the miracle of
"squaring the circle"—a metaphorical expression for regeneration. . . .[8]

A Master Mason, then, in the full sense of the term, is
no longer an ordinary man, but a divinized man; one in
whom the Universal and the personal consciousness
have come into union.[9]

Again, the squaring of the circle—that problem which
has baffled so many modern mathematicians—is an occult expression signifying that Deity, symbolized by the
all-containing circle, has attained form and manifesta-
tion in a "square" or human soul. It expresses the mystery of the Incarnation, accomplished within the personal soul.[10]

While regeneration supposedly occurs to a certain extent
in each of the degrees, the Holy Royal Arch Degree is said to
provide the Mason with a supernatural experience! This experience is so great, it is deemed equal to the Christian meeting Christ. Once again, we quote Wilmhurst:

Moreover, if the Royal Arch be the symbolic representation of a supreme experience attained and attainable
only in sanctity and by the regenerate, it follows that the
Craft Degrees leading up to and qualifying for it will take
on a much deeper sense than they commonly receive
and must be regarded as solemn instructions in the req-
uisite preparation for that regenerate condition. The
Craft work is unfinished without the attainment forth-
shadowed in the Royal Arch. That attainment in turn is
impossible without the disciple of the preliminary la-

bours, the purification of mind and desire, and that crucifixion unto death of the self-will which constitute the tests of merit qualifying for entrance to that Jerusalem which has no geographical site and which is called the "City of Peace" because it implies conscious rest of the soul in God. For many, the suggestion that the attainment of such a condition is possible or thinkable whilst we are still here in the flesh may be surprising or even incredible. But such doubt is unwarranted, and the Masonic doctrine negates it.[11]

It is then that the Mystery is consummated. The Great Light breaks. The Vital and Immortal Principle comes to self-consciousness in Him. The Glory of the Lord is revealed to and in him, and all his flesh see it.[12]

The condition is attained by the illumined candidate is the equivalent of what in Christian theology is known as Beatific Vision and in the East as Samadhi.[13]

The very language and terms of Freemasonry reveal that the Masonic Lodge betrays the message of Jesus Christ and the regenerating work of the Holy Spirit. The symbolic terms of Freemasonry replace the Biblical work of Christ. The following excerpt is a definition of regeneration as given by Dr. Albert G. Mackey:

Regeneration: In the Ancient Mysteries the doctrine of regeneration was taught by symbols; not the theological dogma of regeneration peculiar to the Christian church, but the philosophical dogma as a change from death to life—a new birth to immortal existence. Hence, the last day of the Eleusinian mysteries, when the initiation was completed, was called, says Court de Geneblin (M.P. iv. 322) the day of regeneration. This is the doctrine in the Masonic mysteries, and more especially in the symbolism of the third degree. We must not say that the Mason is regenerated when he is initiated, but that he has been indoctrinated into the philosophy of the regeneration, or the new birth of all things—of light out of darkness, or of life out of death, of eternal life out of temporal death.[14]

Is it not clear this is a definite imitation of the Christian's experience of regeneration? The Masonic Lodge presents the candidate with a counterfeit "new birth"!

[1] Taylor, *Indiana Monitor*, p. 47.
[2] Ibid., p. 121.
[3] A. G. Mackey, *A Lexicon of Freemasonry*, pp. 466–467.
[4] Ibid., pp. 54, 55.
[5] Newton, *Michigan Monitor*, p. 9. See also Taylor, "Badge of a Mason," *Indiana Monitor*, p. 61.
[6] Hall, *The Lost Keys*, pp. 92, 54, 55.
[7] Wilmhurst, *The Meaning of Freemasonry*.
[8] Ibid., p. 139.
[9] Ibid., p. 146.
[10] Ibid., p. 147.
[11] Ibid., p. 166.
[12] Ibid., p. 154.
[13] Ibid., p. 155.
[14] Mackey, *Encyclopedia of Freemasonry*, Vol. II, p. 615.

Masonry, Mormonism and Witchcraft

To state that Masonry participates in the worship of Lucifer would bring questions and doubts from some Christians who are Masons. Yet, it is true. Evidence will show that the Mormon church was begun by a Mason and that there are unusual similarities between Masonry, Mormonism and witchcraft.

Masonry and Mormonism

Two paragraphs from Van Baalen's *The Chaos of Cults* reveal the interesting connection between Masonry and Mormonism:

"The Mormon prophet" Joseph Smith, Jr., was born on December 23, 1805, in Sharon, Vermont. He was reared in ignorance, poverty and superstition. Moreover, he was indolent in his youth. However, quite in keeping with the superstitious atmosphere in which he breathed, he claimed to have visions and divine revelations as early as 1820 and 1823. In the latter year the angel Moroni revealed to him the spot where golden plates lay buried containing the history of ancient America in "reformed-Egyptian caractors." Smith undoubtedly meant CHARACTERS, but, unlike Mother-Eddy, he had never known enough grammar for it to be "eclipsed" by a divine revelation; hence he made occasional grammatical and spelling errors.

In 1830 "Joe," as he was known, organized the "Church of Jesus Christ of Latter-Day Saints" at Fayette, New York. This he accomplished after having convinced a few friends that his "translation" of the Golden Plates—afterward duly returned into the hands of the angel Moroni—had been done, not, as was maliciously slandered, with the aid of a "peepstone in a hat," but with the assistance of the proper "Urim and Thummim" which have been hidden in the earth from the year 420 of our era until September 22, 1823, when "Joe Smith" discovered them in the "Hill Cumorah"; and yet the Book of Mormon, being a faithful rendering of the said plates, gives extensive quotations from the Bible in—the King James Version (1611)! It contains modern phrases and ideas that could not have been known to its supposed author in A.D. 420. It puts the words of Jesus (though often twisted) into the mouths of men alleged to have lived centuries before Christ. It was not only written in a poor imitation of Biblical style; it also undermines the Bible by declaring it INSUFFICIENT, BY ADDING TO AND CHANGING MANY Biblical passages, "by divine revelation." For such reasons as these it could hardly have been revealed by an angel. Its story of the ancient inhabitants of America, the supposed ancestors of the "Latter-Day Saints," [sic] contains twelve historical errors.[1]

The movement began to grow numerically, and through "revelation" the prophet said he was told to move to Missouri. They maintained offices in Kirtland, Ohio, and Zion, Missouri. Several accusations against them were made—they were charged with various crimes—and the governor of Missouri asked them to leave the state. They transported to Illinois, where

Finding welcome in Illinois, they erected the city of "Nauvoo." Here our prophet made his biggest display, announcing himself, among other feats, candidate for presidency of the United States. Accused of gross immorality, counterfeiting, sheltering criminals in the act of fleeing from justice, and other misdeeds, Smith was arrested, but a mob stormed the jail and shot to death both prophet Smith and his brother Hyrum.[2]

When Joseph Smith was killed by the mob, a "Jupiter Talisman" was found on his body. A Jupiter Talisman is associated with occult powers. His mother identified it as his "Masonic Jewel."

In his presidential address before the Mormon History Association on April 20, 1974, Dr. Reed Durham (at that time Director of the Latter Day Saints Institute of Religion at the University of Utah) disclosed some startling information about Joseph Smith that confirms our appraisal and almost cost Dr. Durham his membership in the church:

"...I should like to initiate all of you into what is perhaps the strangest, the most mysterious, occult-like esoteric, and yet Masonically oriented practice ever adopted by Joseph Smith....

"All available evidence suggests that Joseph Smith the prophet possessed a magical Masonic medallion, or talisman, which he worked during his lifetime and which was evidently on his person when he was martyred...."[3]

Hyrum and Joseph both were Masons, and it can clearly be demonstrated that the Mormon church began on Masonic foundations.

Here are the words of a former president of the Mormon History Association:

To begin with, Masonry in the church had its origin prior to the time Joseph Smith became a Mason. Nauvoo was not its genesis. It commenced in Joseph's home when his older brother, Hyrum, received the first three degrees of Masonry in Mount Moriah Lodge No. 112 of Palmyra, New York, at about the same time that Joseph was being initiated into the presence of God and angels and was being entrusted with the sacred gold plates.

By the end of 1832, Joseph had welcomed new brethren, along with their influences into the church. Men such as, W. W. Phelps, Brigham Young, Heber C. Kimball, and Newel K. Whitney, each of whom had been deeply involved in Masonry.[4]

At the instigation of John C. Bennett, George W. Harris, John Parker, Lucius Scovil, as well as other Mormon Masons residing at Nauvoo, and certainly with the approval of the hierarchy of the Church, the institution of Masonry commenced.

Joseph and Sidney were inducted into formal Masonry at Sight, on the same day upon which the Illinois Grand Master Mason. . . Abraham Jonas officially installed the Nauvoo Lodge. It was on March 15, 1842. On the next day, both Sidney and Joseph advanced to the Master Mason Degree.

In only a few years, five Mormon Lodges were established, several others in planning, a Masonic Temple constructed and the total membership of Mormon fraternal brethren was over 1,366.[5]

On April 20, 1974, the Annual Convention of the Mormon History Association was held at the Nauvoo Hotel in Nauvoo, Illinois. At that convention, as we have noted on page 53, a speech was given which has proved to be one of the most revealing events concerning Mormonism. The outgoing president, Dr. C. Reed Durham, Jr., gave his traditional presidential address. In his speech, he identified the similarities of Mormonism and Masonry and recognized that his church had its roots in Freemasonry. Dr. Durham stated it could not be denied that the Masonic Legend of Enoch is the same as that which Joseph Smith wove into the Temple ceremonies.

> The parallels (to the legend of Enoch) of Joseph Smith and the history of Mormonism are so unmistakable that to explain them only as coincidence would be ridiculous.[6]

The similarities of the Masonic Legend of Enoch and Joseph Smith's presentation have been well analyzed in *The God Makers*, which is an excellent exposé of the Mormon church written by Ed Decker and Dave Hunt.

> In the legend, Enoch was 25 years old "when he received his call and vision," as was Joseph Smith "when he brought forth his sacred record." Enoch's vision was

of a hill containing a vault prepared for "sacred trea-sures," on which he saw the identifying letter "M"; while Joseph Smith was led by an "angel" whose name began with "M" to a similar hill containing an under-ground vault (like Enoch's) filled with "sacred trea-sures." Part of the treasures revealed to Enoch were gold and brass plates engraved with Egyptian hieroglyphics giving the history of the world and ancient mysteries of God. Enoch's treasure also included a metal ball [sic], a priestly breastplate and the fabeled "Urim and Thum-mim"—precisely the same objects that were found by Jo-seph Smith along with the gold plates.

If the above sound like an impossible coincidence, there is more. Joseph Smith often referred to himself in his "revelations" as "Enoch," claiming that he had been given this name by God. The Enoch of the legend was chosen to recover and preserve for mankind the sacred name of God; and Joseph was allegedly chosen to recover and "restore" the everlasting Gospel of God to the earth. Enoch buried the sacred record to preserve it just before a great disaster (the flood), foreseeing that after the deluge "an Israelitish descendant would discover anew the sa-cred buried treasure." Enoch "placed a stone lid, or slab, over the cavity into the hill," exactly as Moroni did in the Book of Mormon when he buried the record as the only survivor of the disaster (great battle) that destroyed his entire nation. Joseph Smith, who recovered this record, claimed to be an Israelite, fitting the vision of Enoch even in this regard.

Of course, in the Masonic legend, it was "Solomon and his builders, the Masons, while building and exca-vating for the Temple of Moriah, who discovered the cavern and the sacred treasure." The legend relates that, like Joseph Smith, they were able to obtain it only after three unsuccessful attempts. Three wicked men, how-ever tried to force "one of the faithful Masons who had discovered the treasure, Hiram Abif or Hiram the Wid-ow's son, to reveal the hiding place and the contents of the hidden treasure." He would not; and as they were killing him, "Hiram with uplifted hands, cried out, 'Oh Lord, my God, is there no help for the widow's son?' This has since become a general Masonic distress call."

There were three faithful Masons who pursued the villains and cut off the head of one of them with his own sword. Dr. Durham ended his disquieting talk by summarizing some of the other "coincidences" involved.[7]

Here are the closing words of Durham's speech:

Can anyone deny that Masonic influence on Joseph Smith and the Church, either before or after his personal Masonic membership? The evidence demands comments.... I do not believe that the Nauvoo story can adequately be told without an inquiry into Masonry.[8]

Masonry and Witchcraft

William Schnoebelen is a unique individual. He and his wife were practicing witches, then became active members in the Mormon church and the Masonic Lodge. Later, they came to know the Lord Jesus Christ as personal Savior and were delivered from their past involvements. He relates some of his experiences in a videotape, *Joseph Smith and The Temple of Doom*.[9] In the tape he points out the association that witchcraft, Mormonism and Masonry have.

In June 1973, Schnoebelen was made an elder in the "Priesthood of Melchisedec," and in July of that same year was "sealed for time and eternity." These terms are normally equated with the experience of one who joins the Mormon church. However, this was the ceremony in which he was initiated into witchcraft! The ceremony was performed in a clearing in the woods at Zion State Park, Zion, Illinois, by the Grand Master of all witches in North America. Later, the Schnoebelens sought membership in the Mormon church and were welcomed as witches and instructed that the temple experience of Mormonism would be the peak of their witchcraft growth. As they went through the temple ceremonies, there were parts Mr. Schnoebelen quoted back to the Mormon temple officials because they were the same ceremonies he had learned in the occult. Those rituals are basically the same as those of the Lodge.

Schnoebelen speaks with authority, having been involved in both witchcraft and Mormonism, and is able to make a just comparison to Masonry. This trinity of evil has markings and ceremonies that are almost identical.

The Talismans

The talismans are symbols and signs which are worn on jewelry and clothing, or placed on buildings and so forth. These symbols are the same in all three organizations. Schnoebelen states, "The Masonic/Satanic symbols are in exactly the right places. The square on the right breast is the symbol in the occult for Lucifer, 'the horned god.' It is the symbol related to the male side of things. The compass relates to the female side of things, and represents the 'goddess, or earthmother.'"[10]

It can be easily seen that the markings on the temple garment, "co-incidently", correspond to this qabalistic breakdown of the right-left. The right breast bears the Square—a symbol long associated with the god of witchcraft because of its angular character and because of its similarity to the phallic objects of idolatry.

The compass is on the left breast, and is related to the goddess of witchcraft, "The Queen of Heaven," Jeremiah condemns. The left is, of course, female, dark and mysterious. This is even related to our cultural heritage. The Latin word for left is "sinister" a word which still has evil connotations. The word for right is "dexter" a word with positive associations.

The compass is associated with this element because the circle is forever associated with the goddess in pagan cultures; and of course the compass is the drafting tool used to describe a perfect circle. Even today's witchcraft, "BOOK OF SHADOWS," talks about the center of all witchcraft mysteries being "the sacred circle's secret point" (quote from Third Degree Initiation ceremony, "THE GREAT RITE"). All through the ages, witches and magicians have worked within the protection of a circle—and supposedly, the mysteries of the circle were taught by the goddess to witches. Thus the Mormon temple garment is magically correct twice.[11]

The Apron

In the Mormon Temple Ritual of Endowment, Lucifer is the elevated person. He presents himself wearing a Masonic Apron. He declares to the initiate that his apron is the symbol of his power and priesthood. In every Satanic Order and in every Masonic Order above the Third Degree the participants wear an apron. The apron is worn to cover the genitals and sexual organs and is affiliated with certain sexual rights. A Luciferian Priest must always wear a green apron if he is to properly officiate. Green is the sacred color of Lucifer.

Lucifer's apron is loaded with Masonic emblems. Each Masonic emblem is related to the Gnostic doctrine that one must sin in order to be good.

The Union of Good and Evil

Common to all three groups is the teaching that we cannot appreciate good without knowing evil. This doctrine is observable in several of the symbols. The twin pillars of Boaz and Jachin speak of this idea. Since black is usually the color of evil and white is the color of good or righteousness, the checked mosaic tile symbolizes the mixture of good and evil.

The following quote verifying Schnoebelen's claim comes from "Instructions To the 23 Supreme Councils of the World," Albert Pike, Grand Commander, Sovereign Pontiff of Universal Freemasonry, July 14, 1889, recorded by A. C. De La Femme et l'Enfant dans la Franc-Maconnerie Universelle, page 588.

> Yes, Lucifer is God, and unfortunately Adonay is also god. For the eternal law is that there is not light without shade, no beauty without ugliness, no white without black, for the absolute can only exist as two gods: darkness being necessary for light to serve as its foil as the pedestal is necessary to the statue, and the brake is to the locomotive.[12]

The Grips and Handshakes

The handshakes or grips stand as one of the common factors between this trinity of evil. In the Patriarchal Grip, the wrist fits between the index and the middle finger of the other person. There is also a grip in which the thumb presses between the knuckles of the index and middle fingers.

The Five Points of Fellowship

When a person is raised to the Third Degree he is instructed that the secrets of Masonry are to be passed only under the condition of the Five Points of Fellowship. That position is toe to toe, knee to knee, breast to breast, hand to back and cheek to cheek or mouth to ear. This method is employed not only by Freemasonry but also by the Church of Jesus Christ of Latter-day Saints. It is the method by which Druid witches identify and greet one another. In witchcraft it has a more sexual connotation.

The Temple Architecture

The Masonic temples, the Mormon temples and the occult all use the same designs on their architecture. Consider the six-pointed Star of David as the symbol of the Antichrist, whose number is 666. There are six points on the star and six angles, and six sides to the hexagon which is formed within the circles. When the point is down it is a symbol of calling down power from Satan to oppose Christ.

The Goat of Mendez

"Within the five-pointed star or pentagram (similar to the Star of David), is the picture of a goat. The goat is a long recognized representative of Lucifer, the Wicked one, "the horned god." This is the symbol of the Eastern Star. The Goat of Mendez is the "god of lust."[13]

The Twenty-four Inch Gauge

The twenty-four inch gauge, a common insignia, is located on the navel and the left knee.

The Grand Hail Signal

When a Mason is in distress he raises both hands above his head and cries, "Oh, Lord, my God, is there no help for the widow's son?" The hands are then lowered to the waist with hands parallel to the ground as a Masonic sign. It is a phrase used in the Third Degree when Hiram Abiff is slain. When Joseph Smith was mobbed and killed in the jail in Illinois, he gave the Grand Hail Signal hoping there were Masons among them who would come to his rescue. That distress signal is employed by Mormonism and the occult.[14]

Grand Hailing Sign. It is not standard from state to state. It is designed to be used by one Mason to signal another in case of emergency. Words can also be given but they can not be given with the sign. Those words vary little from state to state, though it is doubtful how many Masons would know or recognize those words if they were to hear them or need to give them.

I will share with you the Maryland sign and the New York sign so you can see the difference.

Maryland:

—The hands are raised skyward with the elbow forming a right angle (like a movie version of a person being held up)

—The hands are lowered to be in front of the Mason making the sign at belt height with palms down.

New York:

—The hands are raised skyward with the elbow forming a right angle

—The hands are lowered to the side in two separate and distinct motions.

From these brief descriptions you can see that one would not recognize the other in time of need because of the variances. Nearly all Masons do not know what I have just shared with you. I didn't know it until I began talking with ex-Masons in different states. If Masons were to truly be in need when out of their state, it is doubtful the sign would be of much help. It might even confuse matters.[15]

The Blood Oaths

The blood oaths are almost identical among Masons, Mormons and those in witchcraft. Every Masonic Order and every Satanic Order hold the candidate with an oath of death.

The vow of having the throat cut from ear to ear, the tongue torn out and the heart plucked from the breast and other such horrible threats is a common denominator among them.

Three Levels of Obtaining Godhood

Man is a god in the making, and as in the mystic myths of Egypt, on the potter's wheel he is being molded. When his light shines out to lift and preserve all things, he receives the triple crown of godhood and joins that throng of Master Masons who, in their robes of Blue and Gold, are seeking to dispel the darkness of night with the triple light of the Masonic Lodge.[16]

Appendix E shows a copy of Schnoebelen's diagram showing how all three groups progress through three levels to reach "godhood." Also read his words below:

In the Masonic Temple, you are figuratively led from the lower or outer chamber of Solomon's half-built temple (1st degree—"Entered Apprentice"), to the middle chamber (2nd Degree—"Fellowcraft") and finally you are "raised to the sublime degree of a Master Mason" in the Sanctum Sanctorum or Holy of Holies in the temple.

Supposedly, these progressions are based—once again—upon perfect mastery of certain secret signs and grips, although in practice, much leeway is given today. Once in the 3rd degree, the Master Mason supposedly has all the "light" in Masonry he needs to achieve perfection, although he quickly learns that other orders (the Scottish and York Rites in the U.S.) await his attention if he really wants to be "illumined."

It must be noted in passing, that there is supposed once again, to be a veil between the middle chamber and the Holy of Holies of the Masonic (Solomonic) temple. Though most masons are unaware of it, the putative destiny of all Master Masons is to ultimately become gods, like their master, Lucifer supposedly did.

By now, anyone familiar with the LDS temple endowment will see many resemblances with what has gone before.

The Masonic similarities are fairly well known, but

the qabalistic ones are even more damning. The original endowment was given on three levels, with the patrons moving from the Telestial Room to the Terestial Room—through the veil to the Celestial room.

Progress from degree to degree was based partially upon learning certain secret signs and grips and words, just as in the Qabalah and Masonry. Every Qabalistic degree has its "secret name." For instance, the name of the (1–10) degree is "Adonai Ha'Artetz."[17]

To verify and establish what Schnoebelen has said, please notice the writings of the following Masonic author:

In the early Church as in the secret doctrine, there was not one Christ for the world but a potential Christ in every man. Theologians first made a fetish of the impersonal, omnipresent divinity; and then tore the Christos from the hearts of all humanity in order to deify Jesus; that they might have a God-man particularly their own.[18]

Consider the DeMolays

It is evident that the Templars have also influenced Masonry. Even today, the pinnacle of York Rite Masonry is the Knights Templar Degree, and the Masonic order for young boys is called the DeMolays, after the last Grand Master of the Templars. The problem with this is that the Templars were corrupted by their contact with the Middle eastern mysticism of the Arabs and Yetzidis.

They worshipped a mysterious god named Baphomet, said either to be a skull or else a three headed being similar to the Hindu trinity of Brahma, Vishnu, and Shiva. Their initiates were required to trample on crosses, urinate on the host, and even perform acts of ritual sodomy. It is somewhat grisly irony that the Masonic boys' order is named after Jacque DeMolay, who was burned at the stake accused of Satanism and pederasty.

DeMolay was burned along with his knights at the command of Pope and King Phillipe LeBelle of France. Dying he cursed them, and within a year, both were dead! Some historians feel that some of the charges against the templars were exaggerated, but the magical texts indicated that they were still a pretty weird bunch. Much of the current practice of Satanism comes from templar rites.[19]

It is evident that Freemasonry is dedicated to, and participates in satanic witchcraft. These truths are not open to the early degrees of Masonry. We understand why Schnoebelen identifies it as a flytrap because the higher one is elevated in Masonry, the greater he is bound to it. Most Masons are not aware of the history of the Lodge or the meaning of the hidden spiritual innuendos. Behind all of Freemasonry is the "god of this world," who has masterminded an organization to deceive the minds of men and thwart the worship of the God of the Bible. If men can be sheltered from Christ, the Light of the World, this Prince of Darkness will lead them to eternal damnation along with himself.

The Masonic Lodge and the Worship of Lucifer

Lucifer is one of the names of Satan. He is "the god of this world," and he is also the "god of Masonry." It is so sad that many belong to the organization without realizing how they have been deceived.

> The Blue Degrees are but the outer court or portico of the Temple. Part of the symbols are displayed there to the initiate, but he is intentionally misled by false interpretations. It is not intended that he shall understand them, but it is intended that he shall imagine he understands them.[20]

Lucifer is the "god of false worship." Notice how Freemasonry accepts false worship:

> BAALIM—Masonry, around whose altars the Christian, the Hebrew, the Moslem, the Brahmin, the followers of Confucius and Zoroaster, can assemble as brethren and unite in prayer to *the one God who is above all Baalim*, must needs leave it to each of its initiates to look for the foundation of his faith and hope to the written scriptures of his own religion (italics mine).[21]

OSIRIS—Everything good in nature comes from OSI-RIS—order, harmony, and the favorable temperature of the seasons and celestial periods.[22]

Lucifer is named as the god that is worshiped in Masonry:

When the Mason learns that the Key to the Warrior on the block is the proper application of the dynamo of living power, he has learned the Mystery of his Craft. The seething energies of LUCIFER are in his hands and before he may step onward and upward, he must prove his ability to properly apply (this) energy.[23]

That which we must say to the crowd is—We worship a God, but it is the God that one adores without superstition.

To you, Sovereign Grand Inspectors General, we say this, that you may repeat it to the Brethren of the 32nd, 31st, and 30th degrees—The Masonic Religion should be, by all of us initiates of the higher degrees, maintained in the purity of the Luciferian Doctrine.

If Lucifer were not God, would Adonay (The God of the Christians) whose deeds prove his cruelty, perfidy and hatred of man, barbarism, and repulsion for science, would Adonay and his priests calumniate him?

Yes, Lucifer is God, and unfortunately Adonay is also god. For the eternal law is that there is no light without shade, no beauty without ugliness, no white without black, for the absolute can only exist as two gods; darkness being necessary for light to serve as its foil as the pedestal is necessary to the statue, and the brake of the locomotive.

Thus the doctrine of Satanism is the heresy; and the true and pure philosophical religion is the belief in Lucifer, the equal of Adonay; but Lucifer, God of Light and God of Good is struggling for humanity against Adonay, the God of Darkness and Evil.

("Instructions to the 23 Supreme Councils of the World," Albert Pike, Grand Commander, Sovereign Pontiff of Universal Freemasonry, July 14, 1889. Recorded by A. C. De La Rive, La Femme et L'Enfant dans la Franc-Maconnerie Universelle, page 588.)[24]

Any Christian who loves the Lord Jesus and reads the above will withdraw from such an ungodly and satanic organization.

[1] J. K. Van Baalen, *The Chaos of Cults* (Grand Rapids: Wm. B. Eerdmans Publishing Co., 1962), pp. 190–191. The spelling of "Latter-Day Saints" by Van Baalen differs from the present day spelling "Latter-day Saints."

[2] Ibid., p. 192.

[3] C. Reed Durham, Jr., *No Help For the Widow's Son* (Nauvoo, IL: Martin Publishing Co., 1980), pp. 22, 23.

[4] Ibid.

[5] Ibid.

[6] Ibid., p. 27.

[7] J. E. Decker, Jr., and Dave Hunt, *The God Makers* (Eugene, OR: Harvest House Publishers, 1984), pp. 119, 120. The metal ball is not normally recognized as part of the parallel, but the author may have some obscure source.

[8] Durham, *No Help For the Widow's Son*, p. 28.

[9] W. Schnoebelen, *Joseph Smith and the Temple of Doom*, Videotape (Dubuque: Aletheia Ministries, n.d.).

[10] W. Schnoebelen, *Tree of Life—Qabalah Chart* (Dubuque: Aletheia Ministries, n.d.). (Key).

[11] Ibid.

[12] J. E. Decker, *The Question of Freemasonry*, p. 13.

[13] The candidate for the Third Degree is often taunted about "riding the goat." This may have reference to the Great Architect of the Universe.

[14] Harmon Taylor, 32d Degree Former Grand Chaplain has this to say about the Grand Hailing Sign.

[15] Ibid.

[16] Hall, *The Lost Keys*, p. 92.

[17] Schnoebelen, *Tree of Life—Qabalah Chart* (Key), p. 4.

[18] H. R. Taylor, *Freemasonry, A Grand Chaplain Speaks Out*, p. 3. (Quoting J. D. Buck, M.D., *Symbolism of Mystic Masonry*, p. 57).

[19] Schnoebelen, *Freemasonry—Satan's Flytrap?* p. 6.

[20] Decker, *The Question of Freemasonry*, p. 8.

[21] Ibid., p. 7.

[22] Ibid.

[23] Ibid., pp. 11, 12, quoting Manly P. Hall, *Lost Keys of Freemasonry*, p. 48.

[24] Decker, *The Question of Freemasonry*, pp. 12, 14.

Masonic Oaths Are Ungodly

9

Every time a Master Mason enters a Master Mason's Lodge, he recommits himself to Masonry. As he enters the lodge-room he approaches the altar where he took his oaths and his obligations. Before the altar, he presents a Masonic salute as a token of his commitment. He lifts his left hand parallel to the ground as if it were resting on the Bible. He raises his right hand to the right shoulder with the hand pointing upward to the "god of Masonry." Then he holds both hands parallel in front of his body reminding him that his bowels are to be ripped from his body, should he not be true to his commitment. Then in a salute-like fashion, he places his right hand to his throat and draws his right thumbnail across his throat from his left ear to his right ear signifying that if he reveals the secrets of Masonry he will have his throat cut from ear to ear and his tongue torn out by the roots. The oath is one of the most influential parts of the Masonic organization. The importance of the vow can be seen in that each degree has an oath that must be taken. There is a special reason for each degree having a vow. The more degrees a Mason has, the more vows he must take and the more promises he must keep, so the more he is bound to the organization. Masonry wins the candidate at the vow, for it is with the vow that the strongest ties are made.[1] Asking a Mason to deny the oath is like asking the Roman Catholic to denounce the veneration of Mary. There is that binding element which chains the individual to the organization. It is here at the vow that the Christian must stand for the truth as it is in Jesus Christ alone.

Masonic Oaths are Administered under a False Reverence

If there were one word that would best describe the Masonic oaths, it would be deception. This is not meant to be slanderous or harmful name-calling, because many highly sincere people are being deceived. The Lodge is hoodwinking its members through the fallacies of the oaths. In the first place, the oaths are administered under a false reverence. The candidate is brought under the most solemn circumstances and must submit to the most demanding pledges. The atmosphere makes a candidate feel that the oath he is taking is honoring to God. With his hand on the Bible he pledges his very life to Masonry. . . ." I (candidate's name), of my own free will and accord in the presence of Almighty God and this worshipful lodge." The candidate might well ask in his mind, Could anything be more honoring to God than this reverent occasion? However, regardless of how sincere that candidate may be, that vow is not pleasing to God, nor is it honoring in any way to Jesus Christ. There has already been a demonstration that formalism is not what pleases God, but, rather obedience to His Word. "To obey is better than sacrifice," is the teaching of God's Word in 1 Samuel 15:22. God does not honor false reverence. Listen to how clearly and openly God opposes such vows:

But above all things, my brethren, *swear not*, neither by heaven, neither by the earth, neither by any other oath: but let your yea be yea; and your nay, nay; *lest ye fall into condemnation* (James 5:12).

Again, ye have heard that it hath been said by them of old time, Thou shalt not forswear thyself, but shalt perform unto the Lord thine oaths: But I say unto you, *Swear not at all*; neither by heaven; for it is God's throne: Nor by the earth; for it is his footstool: neither by Jerusalem; for it is the city of the great King. Neither shalt thou swear by thy head, because thou canst not make one hair white or black. But let your communication be, Yea, yea; Nay, nay: for whatsoever is *more than these cometh of evil* (Matt. 5:33–37).

The Masonic Oaths Result in a False Fear

The Masonic candidate is also presented with blood threats that vary with each degree. (The vows may vary slightly with time and locality, but the content of the vow is the same.) Dr. John R. Rice, in his book *Lodges Examined by the Bible*, brings to light on page 24 that a doctor witnessed a deathbed confession by a Mason, who with two others had murdered Captain William Morgan for revealing Masonic secrets.[2]

A report concerning Captain Morgan's murder appeared in the summer 1982 issue of the *Christian Cynosure*, in which the author quoted directly from Masonic writers. See Appendix F.

Below are the quotes from Captain Morgan's book, *Freemasonry Exposed,* published by Ezra Cook, showing the penalties involved in the oaths, the first being the Entered Apprentice oath:

> To all of which I do most solemnly and sincerely promise and swear, without the least equivocation mental reservation, or self-evasion of mind in me whatever; binding myself under no less penalty than to have my throat cut across, my tongue torn out by the roots and my body buried in the rough sands of the sea at low water mark, where the tide ebbs and flows twice in twenty-four hours; so help me, God; and keep me steadfast in the due performance of the same.[3]

The penalty involved in the violation of the Fellowcraft oath:

> To all of which I do most solemnly and sincerely promise and swear, without the least hesitation, mental reservation, or self-evasion of mind in me whatever; binding myself under no less penalty than to have my left breast torn open and my heart and vitals taken from thence and thrown over my left shoulder and carried into the valley of Jehoshaphat, there to become prey to the wild beasts of the field, and vultures of the air, if ever I should prove willfully guilty of violating any part of this my solemn oath or obligation of a Fellow Craft Ma-

son; so help me, God, and keep me steadfast in the due
performance of the same.[4]

The penalty involved in the violation of the Third Degree
or Master Mason's oath:

> To all of which I do most solemnly and sincerely
> promise and swear, with a fixed and steady purpose of
> mind in me to keep and perform the same, binding my-
> self under no less penalty than to have my body severed
> in two in the midst, and divided to the north and south,
> my bowels burnt to ashes in the center, and the ashes
> scattered before the four winds of heaven, that there
> might not the least track or trace of remembrance among
> men, or Masons, of so vile and perjured a wretch as I
> should be were I ever to prove willfully guilty of violat-
> ing any part of this my solemn oath or obligation of a
> Master Mason. So help me, God, and keep me steadfast
> in the due performance of the same.[5]

The Lodge places an individual under a horrible threat that
does not please God because it makes a claim to that life which
no human institution should have. It is amazing that anyone
would want to belong to a "social" organization (as many Masons claim) that puts them under such bondage. *That vow is a
vow of murder.* God would not want anyone to be involved in
murder. The claim which the Lodge makes to that life is one
that holds the individual in fear.

> God hath not given us the spirit of fear; but of power,
> and of love, and of a sound mind (2 Tim. 1:7).

Some might question whether the vows are taken symbolically or literally. However, the administration of those vows
is presented literally with the literal consequences.

There are Christians who are being held captive by fear.
They are afraid to oppose the Lodge or reveal any of the secrets
because they have taken these oaths. However, it is here that
the Christian can shout, "Hallelujah!" He is not under such
an oath. The moment a person becomes a Christian, he is set

free from these oaths. As a new creature in Christ he now stands before God, not in fear of revealing a secret, but in joy proclaiming from the housetop what God has accomplished in him through His Son, Jesus Christ. The Christian is no longer led about with a rope around his neck, but now as a child of God he can approach God's throne with all the privileges of His children. Praise the Lord for such a salvation! The Mason may ask, "Why is the Christian Mason not under the oath—did he not swear to God?" In Leviticus 5:4–6, we see how a provision was and is available for such a situation.

> Or, if a soul swear, pronouncing with his lips to do evil, or to do good, whatsoever it be that a man shall pronounce with an oath, and it be hid from him; when he knoweth of it, then he shall be guilty in one of these. And it shall be, when he shall be guilty in one of these things, that he shall confess that he hath sinned in that thing: and he shall bring his trespass offering unto the LORD for his sin which he hath sinned, a female from the flock, a lamb or a kid of the goats, for a sin offering; and the priest shall make an atonement for him concerning his sin.

In the Old Testament the sin offering was only a covering, but in the New Testament the blood of Jesus Christ not only covers sin but takes it completely away! "If we confess our sins, he is faithful and just to forgive us our sins, and to cleanse us from all unrighteousness" (1 John 1:9). Do you want to be in bondage to such an ungodly and horrible system as Masonry? (A note of thanks to Dr. John R. Rice for pointing this truth out in my own life.)

The Oaths are Based upon a False System of Morality

There are some things the Christian cannot do because the Bible openly states that such things are sin. Adultery is an example. In no circumstances are we permitted to partake in such immoral deeds. Adultery is sin in any situation, according to the Word of God. We must obey because God spoke His mind on this subject. The Christian's complete moral system is built upon a revelation from God. Such is not the case with

Freemasonry. As we have already demonstrated, the Bible can be removed from the Lodge, and the organization will function just as effectively. The Masonic system is not based upon a revelation from God but rather upon a "moral" system of its own. In the Master Mason's oath, the Mason must swear that he will not commit adultery with another Mason's mother, wife, sister or daughter:

> Furthermore do I promise and swear that I will not violate the chastity of a Master Mason's wife, mother, sister, or daughter, I knowing them to be such, nor suffer it to be done by others, if in my power to prevent it.[6]

Nothing is mentioned about the *evil* of adultery, just the infraction it might bring to the brother Mason or the Masonic institution. Behavior is measured by the effects upon Masonry. Adultery is forbidden in this perspective only. Nothing is stated about it being sin. The standard of Freemasonry is its own moral code. Christian, upon which standard will you pledge your life—one in which the Bible can be removed, or one in which you can rest assured: "Heaven and earth shall pass away, but my words shall not pass away" (Mark 13:31)?

---

[1] *Philalethes* magazine, Grand Lodge, Iowa, February Issue 1987. October 17, 1985, The Grand Master of the state of Pennsylvania denounced the blood oaths and substituted less offensive oaths. Also the British Masons have denounced the blood oaths as of 1987. However, the blood oaths are in effect in almost every other situation.

[2] See also: Hon. Thurlow Weed, *On the Morgan Abduction* (Chicago: National Christian Association).

[3] Captain William Morgan, *Freemasonry Exposed* (Chicago: Ezra Cook Publications, 1827), pp. 21, 22.

[4] Ibid., pp. 52, 53.

[5] Ibid., pp. 75, 76.

[6] Ibid., pp. 74, 75.

Masonry Belittles the Church of Jesus Christ

10

Salvation through Christ is not obtained by joining a church. Salvation is entirely a gift of God. "He that hath the Son hath life; and he that hath not the Son of God hath not life" (1 John 5:12). This salvation is obtained solely by a personal faith in Jesus Christ as Savior. However, the institution of the local church is an institution ordained of God for the proclamation of the Good News of Jesus Christ. It is all-important in His program for our age in time. It is the object of God's affection, something very dear to Christ's own heart (see Matt. 16:18; Eph. 5:23, 25). There is no other organization equal to it.

But Masonry views the Lodge as having superseded the church. To Masonry, the church's supposedly being outdated and ineffective gave rise to the Masonic organization.[1] In the *Indiana Monitor and Freemason's Guide*, there is a selection on the historical sketch of the Masonic Lodge which shows how the organization developed. Here is a quote taken from the selection dealing with the history of operative and speculative Masonry:

> By 1600, according to the Harleian Manuscript (dated about the middle of the 17th Century), our order had almost completely "severed" its dependence upon the Church and became a refuge for those who wished to be free in thought as well as for Freemasons. It was still Christian—almost aggressively Christian—in its teach-

ings. Not for another hundred years or more and then only partially, did it rid itself of any sectarian character whatever and became what it is today, a meeting ground for men of every country, sect, and opinion, united in a common belief in the Fatherhood of God, the brotherhood of man and the hope of immortality.[2]

The progress with which Masonry found the Lodge maturing above the church is very interesting. First of all, the Lodge was dependent upon the church, then it became a refuge for free thinkers (still affiliated with the church), and now it is completely above the restrictions of Christianity. Again, to the Masonic mind, the Lodge has superseded the church.[3] Observe the following excerpt from *The Masonic Initiation* written by W. L. Wilmhurst, president of the Installed Masters Association of Huddersfield:

It is well for a man to be born in a church, but terrible for him to die in one; for in religion there must be growth. A young man is to be censored who fails to attend the church of his nation; the elderly man is equally to be censored if he does attend—he ought to have outgrown what the church offers and to have attained a higher order of religious life.[4]

Below is another statement which verifies this Masonic teaching:

Masonry, as it is much more than a political party or a social cult, is also more than a church—unless we use the word "church" as Ruskin used it when he said: "There is a true church wherever one hand meets another helpfully, the only holy or mother church that ever was or ever shall be."[5]

The Lodge also claims to be superior to the church in principle:

No institution was ever established on a better principle or more solid foundation; nor were ever more excellent rules and useful maxims laid down than are inculcated in the several Masonic lectures.[6]

The Masonic Lodge claims to be superior to all other institutions. This means that it also claims to be superior to the church, which is founded upon the precious blood of Jesus Christ.

The Masonic principles of practice also demonstrate the view of the superiority of the Lodge, best illustrated by an examination of the practices and teachings in regard to the funeral. At a Masonic burial ceremony, the Lodge reserves the authority over the church. There are many statements from Masonic writers that could be given, but these few from Homer F. Newton will show that the Lodge views the church as something only to be tolerated. When the Lodge is given complete charge of the service, the church is not permitted to take part:

1. It is not proper for a Masonic Lodge to co-mingle in its exercises (funeral or other) with any other society. A Masonic Lodge should have entire charge of the interment service or decline to take part.[7]

2. A Lodge may attend a funeral as a mourner, no matter by whom the ceremony is conducted; provided, however, that it shall not unite with any other organization in conducting the ceremony.[8]

3. When a Lodge assumes charge of the funeral ceremonies, the Lodge only must conduct the service, and no person not a Master Mason shall be permitted to participate.[9]

These quotes are not hearsay—they are taken directly from the Lodge's own manuals. Masons do not consider their services begun until after the church is out of the way. They demand the final word over the dead.[10]

The Masonic services, at a residence, church, grave or elsewhere will take place after all the religious services are concluded and will commence upon the officers taking their place about the casket as provided for the house service.[11]

After the clergyman shall have performed the religious service of the Church, either at the house, church, tomb, crematory or grave, the Masonic services commence.[12]

In the *Masonic Burial Services* book prepared by Robert Macey, we find two quotes which also verify this teaching:

VI. Whenever civic societies, or the military may unite with the Masons in the burial of a Mason, the body of the deceased must be in charge of the Lodge having jurisdiction. The Masonic services should in all respects be conducted as if none but Masons were in attendance.[13]

XVI. After the clergyman shall have performed the religious services of the church, the Masonic services should begin.[14]

After the Clergyman has performed the religious service of the church, the Masonic service should begin.[15]

The Lodge claims priority and demands that the church submit to Masonic authority. Many gospel-preaching ministers have had to take their seat at the funeral services in order that the Lodge may have that final word as they present their false plan of salvation and false promise that the Mason deceased will be resurrected to an eternal, blissful Lodge.

At the burial ceremony the Master Mason deposits the evergreen, and the Lodge responds with the words, "So may it be" or "The will of God is accomplished." Those who believe the Word of God automatically have a problem with this pronouncement because they believe it is certainly not the will of God for any man to belong to such an organization. In addition, God's will is never that any soul should die without Jesus. Second Peter 3:9 states that He is "not willing that any should perish, but that all should come to repentance."

The Masonic Lodge belittles the Church of Jesus Christ by binding its members to an oath that demands the church be given second place.

Furthermore do I promise and swear that I will go on a Master Mason's errand whenever required, even should I have to go barefoot and bareheaded, if within the length of my cabletow.[16]

A Mason is under oath that in helping and doing good for others he will always place a brother Mason in a position of priority. This may appear to be an insignificant matter, but the truth is found in Galatians 6:10: "As we have therefore opportunity, let us do good unto all men, *especially unto them who are of the household of faith.*" According to this verse, we are to give priority to brother Christians. Whose command are we to obey—the Bible's or the Lodge's? By all means, the Bible's! The first duty of a Mason is to obey the Master of the Lodge. The first duty of a Christian is to obey the Lord Jesus through the Bible.

[1] The development of the Lodge is not to be confused with the origin of the Lodge. See chapter 4 on the history of the Lodge.

[2] Taylor, *Indiana Monitor*, p. 16.

[3] Hospital records show that some people list the Lodge as their church.

[4] Quoted in R. T. Ketcham, *The Christian and the Lodge* (Des Plaines, IL: Regular Baptist Press, 1962), p. 5.

[5] J. F. Newton, *The Builders*, pp. 241, 242.

[6] Homer F. Newton, *Michigan Masonic Monitor and Ceremonies*, p. 16.

[7] Ibid., p. 94.

[8] Ibid., p. 95.

[9] Ibid., p. 100.

[10] Because of the ecumenical nature of Freemasonry, these final words may vary in practice and undergo rapid change.

[11] Newton, *Michigan Monitor*, p. 101.

[12] Ibid., p. 102.

[13] Robert Macey, *Masonic Burial Services*, p. 4.

[14] Ibid., p. 6.

[15] Ibid., p. 20.

[16] Morgan, *Freemasonry Exposed*, p. 75.

The Christian Does not Need the Lodge

11

First, the Christian does not need the satisfaction of doing Masonic deeds. There is a great deal of difference in the purposes of divine good manifest in the Christian and "good deeds" done by the Masonic organization. There is no denying that Masonry has many hospitals, orphanages and other charities around the world. But there is a vast difference in the purposes of these things and those which have the purpose of honoring Christ. Masonry is seeking some way of pleasing an impersonal "Architect of the Universe."

> Behind the ceremonies of all Masonic degrees lie a fundamental conception of this world in which we live and man's place in it. It is based on the belief common to all religions and to almost all systems of philosophy that there exists somewhere a Supreme Being who created this world, and of whom all mankind are the instruments and servants.[1]

The born-again Christian has found the way of pleasing the living God, and it is through loving His Son, Jesus Christ, and in submitting to His will. Masonry does good works in hope of earning Heaven. The Christian does good works as a result of the fact that Christ has purchased Heaven for him.

> For by grace are ye saved through faith; and that not of yourselves: it is the gift of God: not of works, lest any man

should boast. For we are his workmanship, created in Christ Jesus unto good works, which God hath before ordained that we should walk in them (Eph. 2:8–10).

Second, the Christian no longer needs the Lodge for social reasons. We as human beings are socially minded—we enjoy being around other people. The Christian no longer needs the social affairs of the Lodge. God has ordained the church as a family; it is here that the finest fellowship in the world can be found. Much is heard about the hypocrites of the church, but they are found also in the Lodge.[2] It is strange that many people who will have nothing to do with church or Christ because of "hypocrites" can somehow ignore the hypocrisy in the Lodge. Listen to their claim:

> Trust is a divine attribute, and the foundation of every virtue. To be good and true is the first lesson we are taught in Masonry. On this theme we contemplate, and by its dictates endeavor to regulate our conduct. While influenced by this principle, hypocrisy and deceit are unknown among us, sincerity and plain dealing distinguish us, and the heart and tongue join in promoting one another's welfare, and rejoice in one another's prosperity.[3]

The Masonic Lodge cannot be built on truth for it does not deem Jesus Christ essential to Heaven. Jesus said, "I am the way, the truth, and the life" (John 14:6). The Lodge can never be built on truth, integrity or sincerity—without Jesus Christ. Here, Christian, is why you do not need the Lodge—you have Jesus Christ.

---

[1] Taylor, *Indiana Monitor*, p. 40.
[2] The voice of Masonry emphasizes the hypocrisy of the church and the purity of the Lodge. See as an example J. F. Newton's book, *The Builders*, pp. 242, 243.
[3] Newton, *Michigan Monitor*, pp. 13, 14.

The Lodge Binds the Believer to Unbelievers

12

God commands His children to be "not unequally yoked together with unbelievers: for what fellowship hath righteousness with unrighteousness? and what communion hath light with darkness?" (2 Cor. 6:14). Adultery is a most repulsive sin. Even the sound of this word rings a note of utter shame and disgrace. And yet, sexual unfaithfulness is no greater a sin than unfaithfulness in the worship of God:

> Lest thou make a *covenant* with the inhabitants of the land, and they go a *whoring* after their gods, and do sacrifice unto their gods, and one call thee, and thou eat of his sacrifice; and thou take of their daughters unto thy sons, and their daughters go a *whoring* after their gods, and make thy sons go a *whoring* after their gods (Exod. 34:15, 16).
>
> What? know ye not that he which is joined to an harlot is one body? for two, saith he, shall be one flesh (1 Cor. 6:16).

It is no more God's will for a Christian to belong to an organization that practices false worship than it is His will to marry a harlot. God's desire is for His people to sever their relationship in such a union:

> Come out from among them. . . saith the Lord, and touch not the unclean thing (2 Cor. 6:17).

Should not a Christian belong to the Masonic Lodge to be a witness for his faith? There are fine people who belong— perhaps even ministers—but listen to the words of the apostle Paul:

> But though we, or an angel from heaven, preach any other gospel unto you than that which we have preached unto you, let him be accursed. As we said before, so say I now again, if any man preach any other gospel unto you than that ye have received, let him be accursed (Gal. 1: 8, 9).

God has given the believer no choice but to forsake the Lodge. To belong is to call those "brothers" of whom God has said, "Let [them] be accursed."

The Mason's Obligation or the Christian's Obligation?

13

One more area to be considered concerning the Mason being bound to the Lodge is,without doubt, the most difficult. It is the problem of turning away from someone or something who or which has provided for some special need. When an organization comes to the aid of a hurting, needy family, it is hard for an individual to renounce it for its beliefs and practices. There is that desire to express appreciation for kind favors received. However, there must be a realization of who has given what:

> Who his own self bare our sins in his body on the tree, that we, being dead to sins, should live unto righteousness: by whose stripes ye were healed (1 Pet. 2:24).
>
> For Christ also hath once suffered for sins, the just for the unjust, that he might bring us to God, being put to death in the flesh, but quickened [made alive] by the Spirit (1 Pet. 3:18).

The Lord Jesus gave His life to bear the judgment for the sinner and has rescued his soul forever from eternal separation from God. The question must be asked, "Who have given most—the Lodge or Jesus?" Then to whom is the obligation? You cannot be true to both, for they are opposite in purpose and nature.

The great apostle Paul knew the struggle—read the third chapter of his letter to the Philippians. The heritage of his past was binding and something in which to boast—until he met Christ. From that moment his life knew no obligation to any other than Jesus Christ. In his address to the Corinthian believers he states:

> What? know ye not that your body is the temple of the Holy Ghost which is in you, which ye have of God, *and ye are not your own?*
> For ye are bought with a price: therefore glorify God in your body, and in your spirit, which are God's (1 Cor. 6:19, 20).

Jesus made it clear that "No man can serve two masters: for either he will hate the one, and love the other. . . Ye cannot serve God and mammon" (Matt. 6:24).

A commitment to Christ must be more than a moral obligation; a commitment to Christ is an expression of appreciation. Paul commended the Thessalonian Christians because they "turned to God from idols to serve the living and true God" (1 Thess. 1:9).

Some think they can turn to Christ without turning from idols. But that is not true. God wants you to turn *to Christ from idols* to *serve* the living and true God.

Paul the apostle loved the Lord Jesus with all his heart, soul and mind. His life was lived for the glory of God. Commitment was more than a moral obligation; it was an expression of his love:

> I am crucified with Christ: nevertheless I live; yet not I, but Christ liveth in me: and the life which I now live in the flesh I live by the faith of the Son of God, who loved me, and gave himself for me (Gal. 2:20).

The Final Argument for a Christian to Withdraw from the Masonic Lodge

14

The preceding pages have been written to help the Mason understand the attitude the Lodge has toward Jesus Christ. The Lodge does not permit the name of our lovely Lord Jesus to be used in its functions. No prayer is to be offered in His name, nor is the truth of His glorious gospel to be preached. He is to be given the same position as Osiris, Buddha, Confucious and even Lucifer. His work of dying on the cross for the sins of men is totally rejected by the Lodge. His resurrection is mocked in the ceremonies, and the truth of His coming again is denied. Heaven (so the Lodge claims) can be obtained without Him. If Christ is not allowed in the Lodge, why would any Christian desire to be united with such an organization?

Rev. Harmon Taylor was the Grand Chaplain of the Grand Lodge of Free and Accepted Masons of the State of New York in 1983 and 1984.[1] His love for Christ and conviction of the nature of the Lodge caused him to withdraw his membership from the Lodge. Here is what he says about the Lodge's view of Jesus Christ:

> Thomas Milton Steward, another Masonic author, in his book, *Symbolic Teaching on Masonry and Its Message*, to support his doctrine quoted favorably an apostate Episcopal minister who wrote (page 177) "Did Jesus count Himself, conceive of Himself as a proprietary sacrifice

and of His work as an expiation? The only possible answer is, clearly, He did not. . . . He does not call Himself the world's priest, or the world's victim."[2]

There are many in the Lodge who claim to be Christians, but how they view Jesus Christ is totally different from what the Bible reveals. This one reason alone should suffice for a Christian to leave the Lodge.

[1] Harmon Taylor, *Freemasonry—A Grand Chaplain Speaks Out*, p. 3.
[2] Ibid.

Conclusion

We plead with all born-again Christians who are united with Masonic organizations to recognize they are in union with the ungodly and to sever their relationships with them. We plead with them to take a stand for the truth that is in Jesus Christ. May the Holy Spirit give wisdom and understanding to them as they surrender their lives to the Savior.

God's blessing is on the life of the person who separates from error. He will not necessarily have brothers in high positions who will help advance vocations. He will not necessarily have earthly gain in any way, but God's blessing on lives for obedience is better. He may be ridiculed and mocked for standing for Christ—perhaps even persecuted or martyred—but wonderful peace can be had knowing that a stand has been taken for Him. There will also be God's help through trials. The obedient believer never endures any hardship that cannot be taken to the Lord.

My prayer is that every Mason will examine his relationship to God and realize that Jesus Christ alone is the way to Heaven. I pray that the truth about the Lodge will be revealed, and those without Jesus Christ will call upon Him. Religion may only be a conscience salve to ease the grinding of a sin-eaten soul, but salvation is a wonderful gift of God through Jesus Christ.

> Neither is there salvation in any other: for there is none other name under heaven given among men, whereby we must be saved (Acts 4:12).

What is Freemasonry?

The fraternity of Freemasonry is the oldest, largest and most widely known fraternal organization in the world. Freemasonry is not a secret society, nor is it an insurance or beneficial society. It is a non-profit organization involved in charitable, educational and civic projects.

Freemasonry accepts men, found to be worthy, regardless of religious convictions. An essential requirement is a belief in the existence of a Supreme Being. It teaches the "Golden Rule." It seeks to make good men better through its firm belief in the Fatherhood of God, the Brotherhood of man and the immortality of the soul.

Masonry has no creed, no priesthood, and no plan for salvation. Neither is it an offspring of any church, ancient or modern. It espouses none of them nor is it subservient to any. While Masonry does require a belief in a Supreme Being, each Mason worships in his own fashion according to his religious faith, whether he be Christian, Jew, Protestant, Roman Catholic, Buddhist or Hindu.

The Masonic Lodge, often known as the Symbolic Lodge, Blue Lodge, or Craft Lodge, receives and acts upon petitions for the three degrees known as the Entered Apprentice, Fellow Craft and Master Mason Degrees.

Masonry does not solicit members. No one is asked to join. When a man seeks admission, it is of his own free will—*he must ask*. A person interested in becoming a Freemason should consult a friend whom he believes to be a Freemason to secure his good counsel and recommendation concerning this important undertaking.

Scottish Rite

The Scottish Rite is one of the two appendant bodies of Freemasonry in which a Master Mason may proceed after he has completed the three degrees of Blue Lodge Masonry. Scottish Rite work amplifies and elaborates on the lessons of the Blue Lodge degrees. As with Freemasonry, Scottish Rite is not a religion, and it is nondenominational.

A Master Mason may achieve 29 degrees—the fourth through thirty-second—in the Scottish Rite. A 33d Degree is bestowed on men who have given outstanding service to Freemasonry or to their communities. The Scottish Rite, sometimes called the "College of Freemasonry," uses extensive drama and allegory to emphasize the messages of its degrees.

York Rite

The York Rite is the other appendant body of Freemasonry in which a Master Mason may proceed to supplement and amplify the Blue Lodge degrees, affording historical background on the work and meaning of Freemasonry.

The York Rite takes its name from the Old English city of York. It is said that Atheistan, a British king, was converted to Christianity in York and that he granted the original charter of the Masonic guilds in that city nearly a thousand years ago. Although the York Rite is not a religion in itself, it does develop themes based on the Christian Crusades.

In the York Rite, a Master Mason may become a member of three bodies—a chapter of Royal Arch Masons, a council of Royal and Select Masters, and a commandery of Knights Templar.

As mentioned in the "Every Shriner Is a Mason" section, a Master Mason must achieve either the 32d Degree Scottish Rite or Knights Templar of the York Rite before he can petition to become a Shriner.

Every Shriner Is a Mason

Members of the Ancient Arabic Order Nobles of the Mystic Shrine for North America are members of the Masonic Order and adhere to the principles of Freemasonry—Brotherly Love, Relief and Truth.

Freemasonry dates back hundreds of years to when stonemasons and other craftsmen on building projects gathered in shelter houses of lodges. Through the years these gatherings changed in many ways until formal Masonic lodges emerged, with members bound together not by trade, but by their own wishes to be fraternal brothers.

There is no higher degree in Freemasonry than that of Master Mason (the Third Degree). However, for those men who would like to receive additional instruction and explanation regarding the allegory and symbolism learned in the Masonic Lodge, the Scottish Rite or the York Rite bodies elaborate on the basic tenets of Freemasonry. Only after a Master Mason has achieved the Thirty-second Degree Scottish Rite or the Knights Templar Degree in York Rite, can he then petition to become a Noble of the Mystic Shrine.

Shriners are distinguished by an enjoyment of life in the interest of philantrophy. The approximately 900,000 member organization has buoyant philosophy which has been expressed as "Pleasure without intemperance, hospitality without rudeness and jollity without coarseness."

Thirteen Masons organized the first Shrine Temple in 1872— Mecca Temple in New York City. They knew they needed an appealing theme for their new Order, so they chose the Arabic (near East) theme. The most noticeable symbol of Shrinedom is the distinctive red fez that all Shriners wear at official functions.

Shriners are men who enjoy life. They enjoy parades, trips, circuses, dances, dinners, sporting events and other social occasions together. Furthermore, Shriners support what has become known as the "World's Greatest Philanthropy," Shriners Hospital for Crippled Children.

Through fellowship and philanthropy, Shrinedom strengthens the soul and adds inner-meaning to daily life. It thus spreads a glow of joy through one's entire family.

Men from all walks of life and all levels of income find fun, fellowship and relaxation in their individual Shrine Temples and its activities. There are also regional Shrine Clubs in many communities, family picnics, dances and scheduled trips to near and far—just to mention a few of the activities available.

For the Noble desiring even more activity, there are various Units that he can join, such as: drum & bugle corps, Oriental bands, motor patrols, and clown units. Every effort is made to be sure a Noble has a variety of activities from which he may choose.

There are 185 Shrine Temples located in the United States, Canada, Mexico, and the Panama Canal Zone. And there are informal Shrine Clubs located all around the world.

Throughout its history, the Shrine has always been involved in charitable endeavors. However, in the early 1920's, the membership decided to develop and support an official philanthropy.They fulfilled this desire in the establishment of Shriners Hospitals for Crippled Children.

Today, the Shrine operates 19 orthopaedic hospitals and three burn institutes where children (up to their 18th birthday), regardless of race, religion or relationship to a Shriner, receive excellent medical care. . . absolutely free.

Since 1922, Shriners have substantially improved the quality of life for more than 280,000 crippled and burned children. Millions more have benefited as recipients of treatments and techniques developed at Shriners Hospital.

(from the Grand Rapids Press,
Grand Rapids, Michigan)

Appendix B

Masonic Presidents

	Presidential Term
George Washington Fredericksburg Lodge, Fredericksburg, Virginia	1789–1797
Thomas Jefferson Charlottesville Lodge #90, Charlottesville, Virginia	1801–1809
James Madison Hiram Lodge, Westmoreland County, Virginia	1809–1817
James Monroe Williamsburg Lodge #6, Williamsburg, Virginia	1817–1825
Andrew Jackson Harmony Lodge #1, Nashville, Tennessee	1829–1837
James Knox Polk Lodge #31, Columbia, Tennessee	1845–1849
James Buchanan Lodge #43, Lancaster, Pennsylvania	1857–1861
Andrew Johnson Greenville Lodge #119, Greenville, Tennessee	1865–1869
James A. Garfield Magnolia Lodge #20, Columbus, Ohio	3/4/1881 to 9/19/ 1881
William McKinley Hiram Lodge #21, Winchester, Virginia	1897–1901

Theodore Roosevelt 1901–1909
  Matinecock Lodge #806, Oyster Bay, New York

William Howard Taft 1909–1913
  Occasional Lodge, Cincinnati, Ohio

Warren Gamaliel Harding 1921–1923
  Marion Lodge #70, Marion, Ohio

Franklin Delano Roosevelt 1933–1945
  Holland Lodge #8, New York City

Harry S. Truman 1945–1953
  Belton Lodge #450, Missouri

Gerald R. Ford 1974–1977
  Malta Lodge #465, Grand Rapids, Michigan

Copied from a Masonic Bible, HEIRLOOM BIBLE PUBLISHERS, Wichita, Kansas, copyright 1971

Appendix C

The Masonic Lodge Room

The picture below is of an actual Masonic Lodge as it appeared in the newspaper Monday, September 27, 1982. Notice the large "G" and the Masonic "All-seeing Eye" on the eastern wall. The Worshipful Master resides in the east under the "G," but no one sits inside the northern wall. Also observe the altar in the center of the room, around which the rite of "circumambulation" occurs, symbolizing the "Point within a circle."

Appendix D

The following are used by all three groups: the Masonic Lodge, Mormonism and witchcraft.

MASONIC TALISMAN

Satanic symbols are also used by the Mormon Church

THE MASTER MASON'S GRIP

The Resurrection grip of The Lion's Paw

THE MASONIC APRON

The white lamb skin apron is a counterfeit righteousness. The Masonic Apron is used similarily in all three groups.

THE MOSAIC TILE FLOOR

As black and white are mixed so good and evil must be mixed. Good is not appreciated without evil.

THE FIVE POINTS OF FELLOWSHIP

Passing the Masonic Secret Word for the Third Degree Mah-Hah-Bone

THE SATANIC GOAT OF MENDEZ

The sign of The Eastern Star. The Goat of Mendez is the "god of lust."

Appendix E

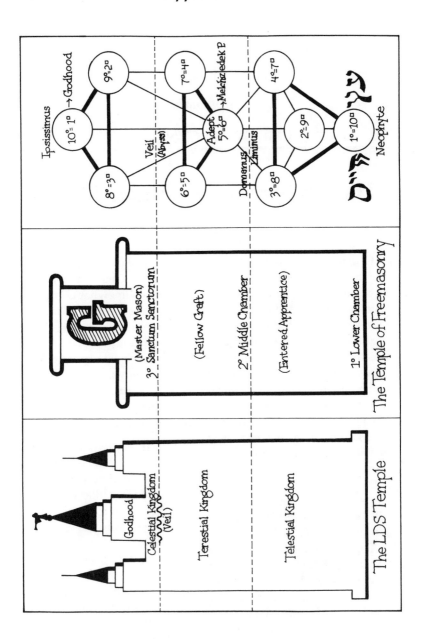

The Temple of Freemasonry

- (Master Mason)
- 3° Sanctum Sanctorum
- (Fellow Craft)
- 2° Middle Chamber
- (Entered Apprentice)
- 1° Lower Chamber

The LDS Temple

- Godhood
- Celestial Kingdom (Veil)
- Terestial Kingdom
- Telestial Kingdom

Ipsissimus

10° = 1° → Godhood

9° = 2°

8° = 3°

7° = 4° → Melchizedek P

Veil (Abyss)

Adept 5° = 6°

6° = 5°

4° = 7°

Dominus Liminus

2° = 9°

3° = 8°

1° = 10°

Neophyte

The Abduction of William Morgan

On a murky night in September 19, 1826, an event took place in Batavia, New York, which shook the nation and which is remembered even today. On that night Capt. William Morgan was abducted for threatening to expose the secrets of the Masonic Order and drowned in the Niagara River. This event might long have been forgotten except that the Masonic Lodge makes a boast of it that it never changes, the same hideous oaths of secrecy, together with the identical atrocious penalties attached, are still required of every person who joins the Masonic Lodge today.

The following is a verbatim transcript of the Masonic version of what took place, taken from Coils **Masonic Encyclopedia**, Article: The Morgan Affair, pp. 423–427, Macoy Publishing & Masonic Supply Company, 34

West 33rd Street, New York, N.Y., 1961. Due to its length the article is somewhat abbreviated as indicated. At the conclusion Dr. Henry Wilson Coil, 33, appends this note: "The foregoing article has been written with the advice and assistance of William L. Cummings, who spent more than 20 years investigating the facts."

THE MORGAN AFFAIR

As early as March 1826, a conspiracy existed between Morgan and David C. Miller to print and sell the Masonic ritual. Morgan was to be the author and Miller the printer. . . Morgan registered a copyright for his book Aug. 14, 1826. . . .

The first installment of Morgan's work called **Illustrations of Freemasonry**, was apparently delivered to Miller in July, 1826.

The crisis developed rapidly during the following month. Miller's printing office was discovered to be on fire.... The Freemasons resorted first to efforts to purchase Morgan's manuscript and later to the making of criminal charges designed to keep him in jail....

On September 11, Nicholas G. Chesebro, Master of the Lodge at Canandaigua and one of the Coroners of Ontario County, arrested Morgan in Batavia on the charge of theft of a shirt and cravat from one Kingsley, but Morgan was discharged by the Justice of the Peace at Canandaigua. Chesebro thereupon produced a claim for two dollars due from Morgan to one Ackley and assigned to Chesebro. As the law then permitted imprisonment for debt, Morgan was committed to the Canandaigua jail.

On Sept. 12, 1826, Chesebro, with Loton Lawson and Capt. Ed Sawyer, went to the jail, which was then in charge of the wife of the jailer, Israel Hall, who was absent, and not being able to obtain custody of Morgan otherwise, discharged the claim against him and took him outside, where a carriage and team driven by Hiram Hubbard was waiting. There was afterward testimony that Morgan's hat was knocked off in a scuffle and that a cry of Help! Murder! was heard. But the appearance of John Whitney reassured Morgan, who took a place in the carriage.

The party drove to Rochester arriving on the morning of Wednesday, the 13th, having stopped at Braces, Victor, Mendon and Pittsford, and having been joined at Victor by James Gillis, a Freemason from Pennsylvania. At Rochester, the team of Ezra Platt, a Royal Arch Mason, was substituted for that of Hubbard, and several other stops were made, including one at Wright's Tavern near Lockport, where the party was joined by other Freemasons, notably Capt. Isaac Allen and Jeremiah Brown, Supervisor and afterward member of the legislature. Entering Niagara County, the party was joined by Sheriff Eli Bruce and Carydon Fox and early on the morning of Tuesday, September 14, the party drew up at the home of William King at Youngstown. The trip of about 100 miles was made in some 30 hours.

At this point, which is naturally the one of the most interest, the story becomes clouded, with imagination and fabrication by both Masons and anti-Masons. . . All that is positively known is that Morgan was incarcerated 5 days until September 19th in the old Powder Magazine at Fort Niagara, and during that period there occurred, entirely independent of Morgan, the institution of a new Royal Arch chapter at Lewiston with Col. King as charter High Priest, which brought a considerable number of Royal Arch Masons to the vicinity of Niagara Falls. There is no reliable account that Morgan was ever seen after Sept. 19, 1826. . . .

On October 4, the Miller Press issued 50,000 circulars (so stated but probably overestimated) announcing the abduction and possible murder of Morgan. . . . On the same date, Governor De Witt Clinton of New York State issued a proclamation urging law enforcement, and followed that with a second on the 26th offering a reward of $300 for information as to Morgan's whereabouts. On March 19, 1827, the Governor's reward rose to $1000 for the discovery of Morgan and $2000 for the conviction of his abductors. At the insistence of Governor Clinton, the Governor of Upper Canada offered a reward of $50 for information about Morgan.

Wild stories circulated as to the various ways in which Morgan was supposed to have met his death. . . . Edward Giddins, a Freemason and custodian of the Fort Niagara unused Powder Magazine, stated that he acted as ferryman to take a party into the Niagara River where Morgan was thrown overboard with his hands tied. . . .

On Oct. 7, 1827, about a year after Morgan's disappearance, a body was washed ashore upon the shore of Lake Ontario. . . . A coroner's jury quickly decided that it was the body of some unknown person and not Morgan's, but at the insistence of Thurlow Weed of Rochester, David C. Miller, and Mrs. Morgan, it was disinterred and submitted to a second coroner's inquest with the result that the body was held to be that of Morgan and his death was attributed to drowning. . . .

In due time, indictments were returned against all those directly implicated in the abduction of Morgan but, since there was no evidence that Morgan was dead (the testimony of Giddins that he saw him drowned evidently repudiated), these were all for kidnapping, conspiracy to kidnap, false imprisonment, assault and battery. Five cases were tried between 1828 and 1831, of which 3 were at Canandaigua, one at Batavia and one at Lockport. Nicholas Chesebro, Edward Sawyer, Loton Lawson and John Sheldon pleaded guilty of kidnapping and were sentenced to jail for one year, one month, and three months respectively. In another case, 10 defendants, including Hubbard, were found guilty on a verdict directed by the court. Orasmus Turner and Jared Darrow were found not guilty, but Eli Bruce (who had been relieved from office by Governor Clinton) was convicted and sentenced to 28 months in jail. . . . Kidnapping was not a felony in New York at that time.

In 1882 the National Christian Association, at a cost of

LINCOLN CHRISTIAN COLLEGE AND SEMINARY

$20,000, raised by solicitation in 26 states and Canada, erected a monument to Morgan's memory at Batavia. It consists of a base and a column surmounted by a statue intended to resemble William Morgan, the whole being 40 feet high and having on the four sides the following inscriptions:

"Sacred to the memory of Wm. Morgan, a Capt. in the War of 1812, a Respectable Citizen of Batavia and a Martyr To the Freedom of Writing, Printing and Speaking the Truth. He was abducted From near this spot in the year 1826 by Free Masons And Murdered for revealing the Secrets of their Order. ***** Erected by Volunteer Contributions from over 200 Persons residing in Canada, Ontario, and twenty-six of the United States and Territories. ***** 'The bane of our Civil Institutions is to be found in Masonry, Already Powerful, and daily becoming more so ***** I owe to my Country an Exposure of the Dangers.' Capt. William Morgan ***** The Court records of Genesee County and the files of the Batavia Advocate Kept in the Recorder's Office Contain the History of the events that caused The Erection of this Monument."

(An extensive bibliography, from 1811 to 1934, on Freemasonry in Batavia and on the Morgan abduction is included.)

Coil's **Masonic Encyclopedia**, pp. 423–427.

Appendix G

SOUTH HAVEN DAILY TRIBUNE
Shrine records shocking

Dear Ann Landers: That glowing letter about how much good the Shriners do was only half the story. I believe you were taken in. The issue is not how much money the Shriners pass on to the hospitals they support but how much do the temples keep for themselves.

The Orlando Sentinel did a terrific series on this subject recently. I am enclosing part one. It will tell you all you need to know.—R. L., TIPP CITY, OHIO

DEAR TIPP: Thank you for your letter and part one of the series by the Orlando Sentinel. John Haile, editor of the Sentinel, sent me part two. I was distressed by the information contained in that prize-winning story.

Shrine refers to their hospitals as "the soul of the Shrine" and "the reason for Shrinedom," but the Sentinel cited Internal Reveune Service records showing that although the Shrine is the richest charity in the nation, it gave its 22 hospitals for children less than one-third of the gross collected from the public in 1984. The remainder was spent on food, travel, entertainment, fraternal ceremonies and fund-raising.

The Sentinel reported that in 1985 the Shriners kept a whopping 71 percent of the money raised, about $21.7 million. This went to pay for a range of clubhouse expenses, including the upkeep of private bars, restaurants and golf courses. They also used the money to pay for conventions, travel and entertainment for their 880,000 members and, again, fund-raising.

The Shrine's most lucrative source of income are the circuses throughout the country. They generated about $23 million in

1985, the paper reported. The records show that less than 2 percent, or $346,251, went to the medical care of children. I find this shocking.

In 1922 the Shriners established hospitals for burned and crippled children. Today they operate 19 orthopedic hospitals and three burn centers. I want to make it clear that I have received dozens of letters from readers who have told me they took their children to a Shrine hospital after a terrible accident, the youngsters received wonderful care and not one cent was charged. This an extraordinary testimony and a glowing tribute.

The facts uncovered by the Orlando Sentinel's investigative reporters in no way diminishes services performed by the Shrine hospitals. The complaint is that a great deal of the money that people think is being given to help crippled and burned children never gets there. In all fairness, I want it understood that every penny sent directly to the hospitals is spent solely to help the children.

Thousands of Shriners were appalled when the Orlando Sentinel made its findings known. They had no idea as to the financial workings of their fraternity. To their credit, many Shrine leaders are now demanding that the temples make clear whether fund-raisers benefit the children or the Shriners themselves. Four cheers for them.

Appendix H

Testimony
Rev. Harmon Taylor
Former
Grand Chaplain of the Grand Lodge
of Free and Accepted Masons
of the State of New York

I trusted Christ as my personal Savior in 1957. Following an automobile accident the next summer I was drawn to ask, "Why, God? Why am I still alive?" The clear answer came that I was to serve Him in the Christian ministry.

I studied for the ministry through the United Methodist church and was appointed to my first pastorate in the same month that our first child was born—June, 1966. God answered my prayer that first Sunday in the ministry, "Lord, let me be a good father and pastor to this child my wife is about to deliver." Two years later I was appointed pastor of a church in Hagaman, New York, and sixteen years later to a church in Clifton Park, New York. I left the United Methodist Church voluntarily, preaching my final sermon as a church pastor on our daughter's 21st birthday.

In 1973 I became a Mason. I joined because all of the active men in the church were Masons and my inquiry brought encouragement to join what they said was a Christian organization.

After taking the First Degree, I felt there was something very wrong with their rites. For one thing I was blindfolded. For another a rope was placed around my neck for most of the ceremony. And finally, the oath contained a penalty that went against all I had ever heard in my Christian walk. My church Masons encouraged me, telling me that it was only in fun and that it wasn't to be taken seriously—it was only symbolic. Blinded by this deception I took further degrees till I became a Scottish Rite and York Rite Mason as well as a Shriner.

I rose steadily through the ranks of the Blue Lodge and was Master of Welcome Lodge No. 829 in Amsterdam, New York, in 1980. I received the Master of the Year Award for increasing Lodge attendance by 259% over the previous year. In 1983–84 I was consecutively appointed by the State Grand Master as Grand Chaplain of the Grand Lodge of Free and Accepted Masons of the State of New York. The *only instruction* I was given for this position was to never end a prayer in Jesus' Name as it might offend non-Christian brothers. Never mind that it offended me not to pray in Jesus' Name. Scripture declares that "no man comes to the Father but by me."

I shall forever thank God for the day when a Christian brother, Bob Miner, shared with me the inconsistency of the Christian walk with Freemasonry. Behind those rituals I had taken are the most satanic things you could possibly imagine. I mention but a few:

The Eastern Star symbol, according to the writer of the ritual, Rob Morris, is the Goat of Mendez, the god of lust.

The writer of the Masonic ritual as it is used today, Albert Pike, 33d Degree, said that the high of the first three degrees are to be maintained in the purity of the Luciferian Doctrine!

Albert Pike, 33d Degree, on page 819 of his book *Morals & Dogma*, boldly declares that the holders of the first three degrees are **intentionally deceived**. It is not intended, he writes, that they shall obtain knowledge but that they shall **imagine** they have obtained knowledge.

Also in *Morals & Dogma* this same 33d Degree Mason describes the eating of bread and wine (Christian communion) as the consuming of the bodies of the dead.

In still another writing of Albert Pike, 33d Degree, he refers to the New Testament as a monstrous absurdity.

You must also know that Albert Pike is not just any man. He is buried in the House of the Temple, the shrine of Scottish Rite Masonry for the Southern Jurisdiction located in Washington, D.C. That is not a mere coincidence. His body was exhumed from its resting place in Virginia and moved to its present resting spot. This required an Act of Congress to accomplish! This man is *the* ranking Masonic authority by virtue of the respect they show for his earthly remains and his books which have been printed under the authority of the Scottish Rite.

Overwhelmed by what I heard, I fled Freemasonry that same day, in November of 1984. Was I right to do that? You be the judge as the next day's events should abundantly convince you. The Lord healed my back of Paget's Disease and I no longer needed to wear the back brace I had worn since being diagnosed with the disease two weeks before my Grand Chaplain apron presentation. The first day out of Freemasonry I was the only one permitted to speak before the Saratoga County Board of Supervisors against continued funding of abortion-peddling Planned Parenthood. The words God gave me were enough to turn the supervisors' hearts from a six year funding practice and they have maintained that stance to this day. This is a first in the nation according to the National Right to Life organization!

Since leaving Freemasonry I have ministered extensively to Christians caught in the Masonic deception. . . We worked with Intercessors for America who helped expose a misleading New York Masonic membership campaign in the news media. Denominations that have since supported our approach include The British Methodist Church and the state Church of England in whose membership is the Duke of Kent, the Grand Master of England.

I renounced my ordination in the United Methodist Church in June 1987 and with it the Masonic headship of the church Board of Ministry who is a 33d Degree "minister" of the United Methodist Church. My ordination has since been recognized by the Conservative Congregational Christian Conference and I minister as International Director of HRT Ministries, Inc. a not-for-profit corporation dedicated to exposing the cult of Freemasonry and other cults that are accepted within the pulpit and pews of many mainline denominations. In the last seventeen months this ministry has seen 524 Christians in Freemasonry. They have fled from every state in the U.S.A. and thirteen countries besides. Praise the Lord! Our major task in this ministry is to stay out of God's way and yet do all He commands.

We are presently presenting seminars in churches and ministering in ever creative ways to Freemasons that they might know the Truth and that the Truth might set them free! . . .

Requests for a catalog of biblically based information on Freemasonry as well as for seminars may be addressed to:

Pastor Harmon Taylor, International Director
HRT Ministries, Inc.
Box 12
Newtonville, NY 12128-0012

Appendix I

Doctrinal Conflicts

The following pages show, in chart form, conflicts between the Masonic Lodge and Bible doctrine.

Doctrine	WORSHIP OF GOD	LUCIFER
Qualities	God will accept worship only when it is based on the Person and work of Christ.	Lucifer is described in the Bible as a wicked fallen angel. He is opposed to God and is an enemy of the Christian.
Bible Doctrine	John 14:6: "Jesus saith unto him, I am the way, the truth, and the life: no man cometh unto the Father, but by me." John 10:1: "Verily, verily, I say unto you, He that entereth not by the door into the sheepfold, but climbeth up some other way, the same is a thief and a robber." Leviticus 10 records how God judged Nadab and Abihu for wrong worship.	Isaiah 14:12–14: "How art thou fallen from heaven, O Lucifer, son of the morning! how art thou cut down to the ground, which didst weaken the nations! For thou hast said in thine heart . . . I will exalt my throne above the stars of God . . . I will be like the most High." 1 Peter 5:8: "Be sober, be vigilant; because your adversary the devil, as a roaring lion, walketh about, seeking whom he may devour."
Qualities	Masonry believes God is worshiped in every religion and that God accepts every religion.	Worship of Lucifer is acceptable. Masonic philosophy is that black compliments white, sin compliments evil—Lucifer is needed by God.
Masonic Doctrine	"A man is a Mason, 'When he finds good in every faith that helps any man lay hold of divine things, that sees majestic meanings in life, whatever the name of that faith may be." "Masonry, around whose altars the Christian, the Hebrew, the Moslem, the Brahmin, the followers of Confucius and Zoroaster, can assemble as brethren and unite in prayer to the one God who is above all Baalim, must needs leave it to each of its initiates to look for the foundation of his faith and hope to the written scriptures of his own religion."	"Yes, Lucifer is God, and unfortunately Adonay is also god. For the eternal law is that there is no light without shade, no beauty without ugliness, no white without black, for the absolute can only exist as two gods; darkness being necessary for light to serve as its foil as the pedestal is necessary to the statue, and the brake to the locomotive." "When the Mason learns that the Key to the Warrior on the block is the proper application of the dynamo of living power, he has learned the Mystery of his Craft. The seething energies of LUCIFER are in his hands and before he may step onward and upward, he must prove his ability to properly apply (this) energy" (Manly P. Hall, *Lost Keys of Freemasonry*, p. 48.)

Doctrine	GOD	THE SCRIPTURES
Qualities	REVEALED—PERSONAL—SOVEREIGN	INSPIRED OF GOD—SOLE AUTHORITY—SUFFICIENT
Bible Doctrine	Isaiah 43:10: "Ye are my witnesses, saith the LORD, and my servant whom I have chosen: that ye may know and believe me, and understand that I am HE: before me there was no god formed, neither shall there be after me." Jeremiah 10:10: "But the LORD is the true God; he is the living God, and an everlasting king. . ." Deuteronomy 6:4: "Hear, O Israel: the LORD our God is one LORD."	2 Timothy 3:16, 17: "All scripture is given by inspiration of God, and is profitable for doctrine, for reproof, for correction, for instruction in righteousness, that the man of God may be perfect, throughly furnished unto all good works." 2 Peter 1:20, 21: "Knowing this first, that no prophecy of the scripture is of any private interpretation. For the prophecy came not in old time by the will of man: but holy men of God spake as they were moved by the Holy Ghost."
Qualities	UNKNOWN—IMPERSONAL—UNIVERSALISM	SYMBOLIC—MAY BE REPLACED—MISQUOTED
Masonic Doctrine	"Behind the ceremonies of all Masonic degrees lie a fundamental conception of this world in which we live and man's place in it. It is based on the belief common to all religions and to almost all systems of philosophy that there exists somewhere a Supreme Being who created this world, and of whom all mankind are the instruments and servants (Lawrence R. Taylor, *Indiana Monitor and Freemason's Guide*, p. 40). "This founded modern Speculative Masonry on the rock of non-sectarianism and the brotherhood of all men who believe in a common Father regardless of His name, His church, or the way in which He is worshipped. . ." (Lawrence R. Taylor, *Indiana Monitor and Freemason's Guide*, p. 19).	The volume of the Sacred Law is an indispensable part of the furniture of the Lodge. In our jurisdiction it is usually the Bible, but any candidate not a Christian may have substituted for it any other volume he considers sacred; e.g., the Old Testament Koran, Vedas or Laws of Confucius" (Lawrence R. Taylor, *Indiana Monitor and Freemason's Guide*, p. 38). "All truly dogmatic religions have issued from the Kabalah and return to it. Everything scientific and grand in the religious dreams of the Illuminati, Jacob Boehme, Swedenborg, Saint-Martin, and others is borrowed from the Kabalah; all the Masonic Associations owe to it their secrets and their symbols." "The Kabalah alone consecrates the Alliance of the Universal Reason and the Divine Word. . ."

Doctrine	THE CHURCH OF CHRIST	THE NAME OF CHRIST
Qualities	A Special relationship of Love and a Unique Union with Christ.	The name of Jesus Christ represents all of power, blessings, authority and glory of God.
Bible Doctrine	Ephesians 5:25–27: ". . . Christ also loved the church, and gave himself for it; That he might sanctify and cleanse it with the washing of water by the word, That he might present it to himself a glorious church, not having spot, or wrinkle, or any such thing; but that it should be holy and without blemish."	Philippians 2:10 and 11: "That at the name of Jesus every knee should bow, of things in heaven, and things in earth, and things under the earth; And that every tongue should confess that Jesus Christ is Lord, to the glory of God the Father."
	Ephesians 3:21: "Unto him be glory in the church by Christ Jesus throughout all ages, world without end. Amen."	Acts 4:12: "Neither is there salvation in any other: for there is none other name under heaven given among men, whereby we must be saved."
Qualities	Masonry has outgrown the need of the church. The Church must be submissive to Masonry.	The name of Jesus Christ is not permitted to be used in the Lodge. Scriptures changed.
Masonic Doctrine	"It is well for a man to be born in a church, but terrible for him to die in one; for in religion there must be growth. A young man is to be censored who fails to attend the church of his nation; the elderly man is equally to be censored if he does attend—he ought to have outgrown what the church offers and to have attained a higher order of religious life."	The Masonic Lodge does not use the name of Christ in prayer or when quoting Scripture as this might offend another Mason who is not a Christian. Here is how they quote 1 Peter 2:5 in the Mark's Master Degree, which is the first degree of the York Rite:
	"Masonry, as it is much more than a political party or a social cult, is also more than a church——unless we use the word church as Ruskin used it when he said: 'There is a true church wherever one hand meets another helpfully, the only holy or mother church that ever was or ever shall be'" (J. F. Newton, *The Builders*, pp. 241, 242).	"Ye also, as lively stones, are built up a spiritual house, an holy priesthood, to offer up spiritual sacrifices, acceptable to God." (The last three words of the verse——"by Jesus Christ"—are omitted.)
		The names of the officers of the Lodge are often blasphemous to Christ. (Potentate, Worshipful Master, etc.)

	THE NEW BIRTH	SALVATION
Doctrine		
Qualities		

Bible Doctrine

	THE NEW BIRTH	SALVATION
Qualities	Regeneration is that work of the Holy Spirit in which man is the possessor of new life in God. John 3:3: "Jesus answered and said unto him, Verily, verily, I say unto thee, Except a man be born again, he cannot see the kingdom of God." Titus 3:5: "Not by works of righteousness which we have done, but according to his mercy he saved us, by the washing of regeneration, and renewing of the Holy Ghost." 1 Peter 1:23: "Being born again, not of corruptible seed, but of incorruptible, by the word of God, which liveth and abideth for ever."	The Christian experiences salvation from the penalty, power and presence of sin by faith in Christ as Savior. Ephesians 2:8 and 9: "For by grace are ye saved through faith; and that not of yourselves: it is the gift of God: Not of works, lest any man should boast." Romans 5:1: "Therefore being justified by faith, we have peace with God through our Lord Jesus Christ." John 3:36: "He that believeth on the Son hath everlasting life: and he that believeth not the Son shall not see life; but the wrath of God abideth on him."

Masonic Doctrine

	THE NEW BIRTH	SALVATION
Qualities	The Masonic Lodge presents a counterfeit new birth, which supposedly equals the Christian Beatific Vision. "In a word, he has become regenerated. He has achieved the miracle of squaring the circle— a metaphorical expression for regeneration. . . ." "A Master Mason, then, in the full sense of the term, is no longer an ordinary man, but a divinized man; one in whom the Universal and the personal consciousness have come into union." "It is then that the Mystery is consummated. The Great Light breaks. The Vital and Immortal Principle comes to self-consciousness in him. The Glory of the Lord is revealed to and in him, and all his flesh sees it." "The conditions attained by the illumined candidate is the equivalent of what in Christian theology is known as Beatific Vision and in the East as Samadhi."	Masonry teaches that salvation is earned by the benefit of the Masonic pass and the results of good works. "Then by the benefit of a pass, a pure and blameless life with a firm reliance on Divine Providence, shall we gain ready admission into that celestial Lodge above where the Supreme Architect of the Universe presides; where standing at the right of our Supreme Grand Master, He will be pleased to pronounce us just and upright Masons; then will we be fitly prepared as living stones for that spiritual building, that house not made with hands eternal in the heavens; where no discordant voice shall be heard, but all the soul shall experience shall be perfect bliss, and all it shall express will be perfect praise; and love divine will ennoble every heart, and hosannas exalted employ every tongue" (Homer F. Newton, *Michigan Monitor and Ceremonies*, p. 42).

Doctrine	REDEMPTION	RESURRECTION
Qualities	Christians have been purchased by Jesus Christ through His work on the Cross and thus are set free.	There are two orders of resurrection. Those who accept Christ as Savior will be resurrected bodily by Jesus Christ at His return. The soul goes immediately to Glory.
Bible Doctrine	1 Peter 1:18 and 19: "Forasmuch as ye know that ye were not redeemed with corruptible things, as silver and gold, from your vain conversation received by tradition from your fathers; But with the precious blood of Christ, as of a lamb without blemish and without spot." Colossians 1:14: "In whom we have redemption through his blood, even the forgiveness of sins."	John 11:25: "Jesus said unto her, I am the resurrection and the life: he that believeth in me, though he were dead, yet shall he live: And whosoever liveth and believeth in me shall never die. Believest thou this? 1 Corinthians 15:55–57: "O death, where is thy sting? O grave, where is thy victory? The sting of death is sin; and the strength of sin is the law. But thanks be to God, which giveth us the victory through our Lord Jesus Christ."
Qualities	Masonry offers a false redemption.	Masonry presents a resurrection from the grave through the Lodge. Masonic burials present a false gospel.
Masonic Doctrine	"By its legend and all its ritual, it is implied that we have been redeemed from the death of sin and the sepulchre of pollution" (Lawrence R. Taylor, *Indiana Monitor and Freemason's Guide*, p. 145).	"The Sublime Degree teaches that in another life it may be found. That is why it is the Sublime Degree" (Lawrence R. Taylor, *Indiana Monitor and Freemason's Guide*, p. 148). "The Sprig of Acacia . . . serves to remind us of that imperishable part of man which survives the grave, and bears the nearest affinity to the supreme intelligence which pervades all nature, and which can never, never, never die. Then finally, my brethren, let us imitate . . . that, like him, we may welcome the grim tyrant Death, and receive him as a kind messenger sent by our Supreme Grand Master, to translate us from this imperfect to that all perfect, glorious, and celestial Lodge above, where the Supreme Architect of the Universe presides" (Lawrence R. Taylor, *Indiana Monitor and Freemason's Guide*, pp. 106, 107).

THE PRINCIPLE OF SEPARATION FROM EVIL

Doctrine	
Qualities	The Christian is to withdraw himself from a union which binds him to unrighteousness.
Bible Doctrine	Galatians 1:6: "I marvel that ye are so soon removed from him that called you into the grace of Christ unto another gospel: which is not another; but there be some that trouble you, and would pervert the gospel of Christ. But though we, or an angel from heaven, preach any other gospel unto you than that which we have preached unto you, let him be accursed. As we said before, so say I now again, if any man preach any other gospel unto you than that ye have received, let him be accursed." 2 Corinthians 6:17, 18: "Wherefore come out from among them, and be ye separate, saith the Lord, and touch not the unclean thing; and I will receive you, and will be a Father unto you, and ye shall be my sons and daughters, saith the Lord Almighty."
Qualities	Masonry traces its history and its orgin to the worship of idols. It is built on a system that approves of the worship of many gods. It is inclusive in its fellowship.
Masonic Doctrine	"It is manifest that Freemasonry has retained heirlooms which in one way or another have come to it out of the abundance of the past. Traces of the earliest form of sun worship are to be found in some of the ceremonials of the Lodge room. Its point within a circle and its five-rayed star were symbols of religious significance in many ancient faiths" (H. L. Haywood, *A History of Freemasonry*, p. 17). "Masonry, around whose altars the Christian, the Hebrew, the Moslem, the Brahmin, the followers of Confucius and Zoroaster, can assemble as brethren and unite in prayer to the *one God who is above all Baalim*, must needs leave it to each of its initiates to look for the foundation of his faith and hope to the written scriptures of his own religion." (Italics by author)27 "Therefore no private piques or quarrels must be brought within the Door of the Lodge, far less any quarrels about religion or Nations or State Policy, we being only as Masons of the universal religion above mentioned" (Lawrence R. Taylor, *Indiana Monitor and Freemason's Guide*, p. 32).

Appendix J

Ecclesiastical Separation

In January, 1987, the Baptist Union of Scotland formed a council to examine the Masonic Lodge.

After thorough research the group produced the booklet, *Baptists and Freemasonry,* which led the Baptist Union of Scotland to denounce the Masonic Lodge. Here is their conclusion to an eleven-page report:

INFLUENCE IN SOCIETY
Whilst this is not strictly within the group's remit, it would be a matter of Christian concern if there were strong evidence that Freemasonry exerts an undue and detrimental influence in certain areas of our national life (e.g. in the professions, industry, local government, Civil service, police). Allegations of unfair advantage, of the distortion of justice and even of corruption, have often been made and as often strenuously denied. Because the movement works largely in secrecy and uses secret signs and code words, it is often difficult to pinpoint specific instances. Some who have recently investigated some of the allegations at depth appear to be convinced that they have some foundation. For example, Sir Kenneth Newman in his guidelines issued to the Metropolitan Police leaves no doubt that in his view Freemasonry and police service are incompatible. Stephen Knight (in The Brotherhood) gives detailed records of his own investigations in various areas.

CONCLUSION
We feel that there is a great danger that the Christian who is a Freemason may find himself compromising his Christian beliefs and his allegiance to Jesus Christ, perhaps without realising what he is doing.

It may be that some entered the movement as young men with a view to possible advantages it appeared to offer or through family connections. It may be that they accepted the strange rites of initiation largely as a means to an end. It could well be that the religious aspects of Freemasonry did not greatly concern them. Hence they may never have been acutely aware of any serious incompatibility between their Christian faith and membership in the Brotherhood.

However, the clear conclusion we have reached from our enquiry is that there is an inherent incompatibility between Freemasonry and the Christian faith. Also that commitment within the movement is inconsistent with a Christian's commitment to Jesus Christ as Lord.

"This is the message we have heard from him and proclaim to you, that God is light and in him is no darkness at all. If we say we have fellowship with him while we walk in darkness, we lie and do not live according to the truth; but if we walk in thelight, and he is in the light, we have fellowship with one another, and the blood of Jesus his Son cleanses us from all sin".

(1 John 1:5–7)

No doubt the charge will be given that this is only one group that has taken a stand against the Lodge. But the Baptist Union of Scotland also reported other churches finding fault with Masonry.

APPENDIX 3
REPORTS FROM OTHER DENOMINATIONS
Most of the reports and comments available tend to strike the note of quiet pastoral concern, rather than indulging in wild dramatic claims. Certain basic concerns are common to all, and it is surely not without significance that enquiry groups set up by Christians from differing traditions have arrived at very similar conclusions to our own.

The Church of Scotland Panel on Doctrine (1965) concludes, "In our view total obedience to Christ precludes joining any organization such as the Masonic movement, which seems to demand a whole-hearted allegiance to itself, and at the same time refuses to divulge all that is involved in that allegiance prior to joining. . . . The initiate is required to commit himself to Masonry in a way that a Christian should only commit himself to Christ." (They are instituting a fresh enquiry following the discussion in the 1987 Assembly.)

The Free Church of Scotland report concludes, "in the minds of the committee, according to their interpretation of Scripture, membership of Freemasonry . . . is inconsistent with a profession of the Christian faith."

The Methodist report states, "There is a great danger that the Christian who becomes a Freemason will find himself compromising his Christian beliefs or his allegiance to Christ, perhaps without realising what he is doing. Consequently our guidance is that Methodists should not become Freemasons."

The recently published report of the Church of England enquiry points to a number of fundamental reasons to question the incompatibility of Freemasonry and Christianity. They believe that Christians who are also Freemasons face major difficulties in reconciling the two allegiances, and that some of the Masonic rituals are felt to be "blasphemous, disturbing and even evil."

The principle of separation is applicable to churches as well as individuals. We are instructed that the church is to be separate from the binding and sinful relationship of the world. The principle is so clearly set forth in 2 Corinthians 6:14–18.

More and more churches and denominations are vocalizing their refusal to participate with Freemasonry. They give warning to their people in various ways to avoid union with the Lodge. Those opposing the Lodge are not coming from only a narrow section of Christianity, but from a broad and various sector of churches, groups and schools. Here are a few:

General Association of Regular Baptist Churches:

The GARBC is a group of about 1600 churches that have banded together to stand for the truth as it is in Jesus Christ alone. In 1932, the group was formed to oppose the liberalism that had engulfed the Northern Baptist Convention. One of the early leaders of that movement was Dr. Robert Thomas Ketcham. Dr. Ketcham authored a pamphlet, The Christian and the Lodge. While it is not a lengthy paper, it does present the GARBC's opposition to Masonry.

Grace Brethren:

One of the groups that early took a stand on the issues of the Lodge was the Fellowship of Grace Brethren Churches, a group of about 260 churches. Its school is Grace College and Seminary. Dr. Alva J. McClain, first president, wrote a very fine treatise against the Lodge entitled, Freemasonry and Christianity.

Christian Reformed Churches:

This group of about 800 churches represents approximately 310,000 people, and has one of the strongest statements opposing Freemasonry. In fact, it was one of the issues for their origin:

> XV. LODGE AND CHURCH MEMBERSHIP
> Ever since its beginning in 1857, the Christian Reformed Church has taken a position relative to lodge membership. That position has always been one of opposition. In fact, when the denomination came into existence by separating itself from the Dutch Reformed Church, one of the reasons given for that separation was the Dutch Reformed toleration of lodge membership. (See The Christian Reformed Church, John Kromminga, p. 32.)
> Subsequent synodical decisions indicate a continuing and firm opposition to the lodge and membership in the lodge. A report presented and adopted in 1900 is of great importance in understanding the position of the Christian Reformed Church regarding lodge membership.
> In 1974 the study committee on Lodge and Church Membership presented an extensive report to synod. Synod adopted this report, and once more reiterated its firm stand against lodge membership by church members.

The Christian Reformed churches also publish a twenty-two page article entitled Supplement—Report 45. which states the reasons why they oppose the Lodge.

Independent Fundamental Churches of America:

The IFCA opposes membership in the Masonic Lodge. While every church is independent, the fellowship requires a stand against Freemasonry.

The Independent Bible Mission is the missionary church extention of the IFCA, and their constitution states clearly on page 17, Article VII., Section C., Point 2 in the Requirements for membership: (2) Freedom from membership in oath-bound religious or social secret organization. 2 Corinthians 6:14, 7:1"

Lutheran Bodies:

A number of Lutheran synods forbid membership in the Masonic Lodge.

The Wisconsin Evangelical Lutheran Synod (WELS) is one group of 1100 churches and represents 420,000 members. While each local church must declare its opposition to Freemasonry, the synod publishes and produces a great deal of material stating the reason for their stand. For example, they publish *The Anti-Christian Spirit of the*

Lodge by Paul Piper, pastor of St. Peter's Evangelical Lutheran Church. The booklet is published by the Milwaukee Delegate Conference.

The Lutheran Church—Missouri Synod (LCMS)—represents 5900 churches and a baptized membership of 2.6 million people. Their position is similar.

The Evangelical Lutheran Synod (ELS) is a smaller conservative group which consists of 120 churches and 20,000 members.

Presbyterian Church in America:

In 1988, the Presbyterian Church In America (PCA) elected Dr. D. James Kennedy as moderator of the 16th General Assembly assembled in Knoxville, Tennessee. Comissioners to the Assembly representing the 160,000-member denomination took a strong stand against Freemasonry.

Many Are Speaking Out:

How thrilling it is to hear how many are now beginning to reject the hoodwink of Freemasonry. There are even specialized ministries led by men who have been high-ranking officials in the Lodge and because of Christ are forming ministries with the specific purpose of making the truth known and helping others come out of the Lodge.

Free the Masons Ministry: The organization is headed up by Ed Decker, who is the co-author of the well known The Godmakers. Ministering with him is William Schnoebelen. Both of these men are discussed at length in this book. Both are former Masons and former Mormons and write from firsthand experience. They have many good materials available. They are from a more charismatic and Pentecostal background. Their address is PO Box 1077, Issaquah, WA 98027.

In His Grip Ministries, Inc.: Mick Oxley has formed a ministry opposing the Lodge. As a Royal Arc Mason he is well qualified to write on the subject of Masonry. He, too, has materials available by writing to Route 1, Box 257-E, Crescent City, FL 32012.

Pastor Jim Shaw: Another voice against the evils of Masonry comes from this man who is a former 33d Degree Mason. This is the highest recognized Masonic degree in America. However Christ brought him out of the Lodge. His tract, "Out of Darkness into the Light" is a testimony of how he came out of Freemasonry after 19 years of serving the Lodge. He has other materials, as well, which may be ordered by writing to Box 884, Silver Springs, FL 32688.

HRT Ministries: Harmon Taylor, whose testimony is found on page 104 of this book, left his pastorate in a United Methodist church to become the international director of the HRT Ministries. He is a former Grand Chaplain of the Grand Lodge of the State of New York. He is well versed in Masonry and is dedicated to exposing the errors of Free-masonry. His materials can be ordered from PO Box 12, Newtonville, NY 12128-0012.

The John Ankerberg Show: One contemporary spokesman against the errors of the Masonic Lodge is John Ankerberg, a Southern Baptist evangelist who hosts a television program out of Chattanooga. He has produced a series of videotapes of the Masonic rituals. Jack Harris, a former Mason, and several men reenact the initiation rites of the first three degrees of the Lodge. Ankerberg also joins with Walter Martin, an expert on the cults, in interviewing a 32d degree Mason about the compatibility of Christianity and Masonry. The interviews are videotaped and available for purchase. John Ankerberg and Jack Harris both had their lives threatened as a result of his public exposure of the Lodge. Tapes may be ordered by writing John Ankerberg, PO Box 8977, Chattanooga, TN 37411.

John R. Rice: John R. Rice is now with the Lord. He was an independent Baptist evangelist who authored the book, *Lodges Examined by the Bible*. His book made a great impact on the lives of many and helped draw others out of the Lodge.

Now is the time for churches and denominations to vocalize their opposition to the principles of Masonry. Many times Christians are taught that the Lodge and the church are compatible. Unless our voices are raised we are compromising with something that opposes Christ. Churches and denominations must speak out now.

Groups often make public statements concerning the issues of the hour. We publicly oppose abortions, alcoholic drinking, immorality and so on. It is time for groups to state their protest concerning Masonry.

Appendix K

Albert Pike

The only monument to a Confederate general in the nation's capital stands on public property between the U.S. Department of Labor Building and the city's Municipal Building on D Street, N.W., between Third and Fourth Streets. It is a statue of Albert Pike, the grand philosopher of Scottish Rite Masonry, who was indicted for treason for his activities during the Civil War.

Clad in a frock coat and weskit, wearing shoulder-length hair, the bewhiskered Pike is depicted holding in his left hand a volume of *Morals and Dogma,* his great Masonic treatise.

Chiseled into the statue's pedestal are words which purport to describe the man's abilities; poet, author, jurist, orator, philosopher, philanthropist, scholar and soldier. The sculpture gives no indication that Pike, as a Confederate general, was commander of a band of Indians who scalped and killed a number of Union soldiers during the Battle of Pea Ridge (Ark.) [63]

Military records show that Indians at the Battle of Pea Ridge conducted warfare with "barbarity." Adjutant John W. Noble of the Third Iowa Regiment said: ". . . from personal inspection . . . I discovered that eight of the men . . . had been scalped." [64]

Adjutant Noble added that the bodies had been exhumed and many showed "unmistakable evidence" of having been "murdered after they were wounded." [65]

First sergeant Daniel Bradbury swore he was present at the Battle on March 7, 1862 and saw Indians "doing as they pleased." The next day, he saw about 3,000 Indians "marching in good order under the command of Albert Pike." [66]

In a letter, dated March 21, 1862, Pike was admonished by D. H. Maury, assistant Adjutant General of the Trans-Mississippi District "to restrain [Indians under his command] from committing any barbarities upon the wounded prisoners, or dead who may fall into their hands." [67]

The New York Times reported that Pike had "seduced" the Indians into war paint. [68]

Pike was born in Massachusetts in 1809, but moved to Arkansas as a young man where he became president of the State Council of the anti-Catholic American Party.

In 1861, Pike wrote a pamphlet "State or Province, Bond or Free," addressed to the people of Arkansas following Abraham Lincoln's election to the Presidency of the United States, but prior to his inauguration. In the pamphlet, Pike said the border States should at once "unite with the states that have seceded and are yet to secede, meet them in convention, and aid in framing a Constitution and setting on foot a Government."

Then, he continued, there will no longer be a few seceded States, "but a new and powerful confederacy, to attempt to coerce which would be a simple fatuity. A war against it would be too expensive a luxury for the North to indulge in, and would, moreover, defeat its own purpose." [69]

Pike served as Commissioner to the Indians West of Arkansas in the Confederate States of America, and between July 10 and October 7, 1861 concluded Treaties of Friendship and Alliance with seven Indian nations on behalf of the Confederacy. The treaties gave certain tribes the unqualified right of admission as a State of the Confederacy and allowed each tribe a delegate in the Confederate Congress. However, President Jefferson Davis of the Confederacy urged that aspect of the treaties be deleted.

Subsequently, the Comanches were "greatly astonished on being informed that they had made a treaty with enemies of the Government of their Great Father in Washington." [70]

That history of Albert Pike is rarely, if ever, discussed by Masons. He remains to them "an outstanding man," [71] a "great man, . . . a truly universal and creative genius, . . . an inexhaustible mine of inspiration, [and] a mental and spiritual giant." [72]

From *Behind the Lodge Door* by Paul A. Fisher (Washington, D.C.: Shield Publishing Co., 1988), pp. 48–50.

Bibliography

Ankerberg, John. *The Masonic Lodge: Behind Closed Doors.* Chattanooga: The John Ankerberg Show, 1986. Jack Harris Videotape.

Decker, J. E. Jr., and Dave Hunt. *The Godmakers.* Eugene, OR: Harvest House Publishers, 1984.

_____ . *The Question of Freemasonry.* Issaquah, WA: Free the Masons Ministry, n.d.

Durham, C. Reed, Jr. *No Help For the Widow's Son.* Nauvoo, IL: Martin Publishing Company, 1980.

Finney, C. G. *The Character, Claims and Practical Workings of Freemasonry.* Southern District of Ohio: Western Tract and Bible Society, 1869.

Fisher, Paul A. *Behind the Lodge Door.* Washington, D.C.: Shield Publishing, 1988.

A Frank Exposure of Freemasonry. KY: The Baptist Examiner Book Shop, n.d.

Hall, Manley P. *The Lost Keys of Freemasonry.* Chicago: The Charles T. Powner Co., 1976.

Haywood, H. L. *Freemasonry and the Bible.* Chicago: The Masonic History Company, 1947.

_____ . *A History of Freemasonry.* New York: The John Day Co., 1927.

_____ . *More About Freemasonry.* Chicago: The Charles T. Powner Co., 1980.

Hunter, Frederick M. *The Regius Manuscript.* OR: Research Lodge, 1952.

Ketcham, R. T. *The Christian and the Lodge.* Des Plaines, IL: Regular Baptist Press, 1962.

Mackey, Albert G. *An Encyclopedia of Freemasonry.* Vol. 2. New York: The Masonic History Co., 1910.

_____ . *A History of Freemasonry.* New York: The Masonic History Co., 1906.

_____ . *A Lexicon of Freemasonry.* New York: Maynard, Merrill & Co., 1852.

Macoy, Robert. *Masonic Burial Services.* Chicago: Ezra Cook Publications, 1968.

McClain, Alva. *Freemasonry and Christianity.* IN: The Brethren Missionary Herald Co.

McGavin, Cecil E. *Mormonism and Masonry.* Salt Lake City: Bookcraft Publishers, 1956.

Morgan, Captain William. *Freemasonry Exposed.* Chicago: Ezra Cook Publictions, 1827.

Newton, Homer F. *Michigan Masonic Monitor and Ceremonies.* MI: Grand Lodge of Free and Accepted Masons of the State of Michigan, 1937.

Pike, Albert. *Morals and Dogma.* WA: House of the Temple, 1966.

Rice, John R. *Lodges Examined by the Bible.* Murfreesboro, TN: Sword of the Lord Publishers, 1943.

Schnoebelen, W. *Freemasonry: Satan's Flytrap?* Dubuque, IA: Aletheia Ministries, n.d.

_____ . *Joseph Smith and the Temple of Doom.* Dubuque, IA: Aletheia Ministries, n.d. Videotape.

_____ . *The Tarot of the Egyptians.* Dubuque, IA: Aletheia Ministries, n.d.

_____ . *Witch's Sabbat Chart Key.* Dubuque, IA: Aletheia Ministries, n.d.

Stillson, H. L. *A History of the Ancient and Honorable Fraternity of Free and Accepted Masons and Concordant Orders.* Boston: The Fraternity Publishing Company, 1912.

Taylor, Harmon. *Freemasonry—A Grand Chaplain Speaks Out.* Issaquah, WA: The Masons Ministry, n.d.

Taylor, Lawrence T. *Indiana Monitor and Freemason's Guide.* IN: Most Worshipful Grand Lodge of Free and Accepted Masons of the State of Indiana, 1957.

Van Baalen, Jan Karel. *The Chaos of Cults.* Grand Rapids: Wm. B. Eerdmans Publishing Co., 1962.

Weed, Hon. Thurlow. *The Morgan Abduction.* Chicago: National Christian Association, 1882.

Wilmhurst, W. L. *The Meaning of Masonry.* New York: Bell Publishing Co., 1980.

If you are a Mason and have questions or need help concerning your relationship with God or with the Masonic Lodge, you may write to Dale Byers, 06701 Blue Star Highway, South Haven, Michigan, 49090, or to Regular Baptist Press, 1300 N. Meacham Rd., Schaumburg, Illinois, 60173-4888.

Following is a sample letter for receiving a demit from the Lodge if you so desire.

Sample Letter for Receiving a Demit

To my friends and acquaintances in the Masonic Lodge:

This letter is a formal request for my demit from the Masonic Lodge. Please remove my name from your membership rolls and mail to me a copy of my demit.

Thank you for allowing me an opportunity to express my reasons for withdrawing from the Lodge. Do understand that my withdrawal has no personal bearing upon individual members or any personal conflicts with members. Those in the Lodge who are my friends know that I still treasure their personal friendships.

However, I am a Christian and must forsake the Lodge because its teachings are contrary to the true teachings of the Bible. Freemasonry rejects the Lord Jesus Christ Who is the Lord and Master of my life. I cannot with a clear conscience be a Mason because Jesus Christ is not allowed to be named or worshiped in the Lodge as it might offend another Mason. Masonry's respected authors, Albert Mackey and Albert Pike, openly claim that Masonry is a religion. They are right! It is a religion without Christ.

Many of us have heard that the Lodge is based on the Bible. However, in Freemasonry the Bible is rejected and God's Word is misused and misquoted. The Lodge's religion is universalism and the Bible is nothing more than a symbol.

Masonry promises to its members the blessings of Heaven and acceptance before God. The Masonic plan of salvation is totally contrary to what the Bible teaches. Men cannot be saved apart from Jesus Christ as Savior.

In closing, may I express my love for you as individuals and if you desire, I will gladly share how I became a Christian and help you to understand how you, too, may become a follower of Jesus Christ.

Your friend in Christ,

LINCOLN CHRISTIAN COLLEGE AND SEMINARY

MAS
+
366.1097
B9935

128050

LINCOLN CHRISTIAN COLLEGE AND SEMINARY

3 4711 00218 4929